T0196619

The Story
and Teachings of
JANNIE B. JOHNSON

Formed by God and Called to Teach

MAMIE B. CROCKETT

WESTBOW
PRESS®
A DIVISION OF THOMAS NELSON
& ZONDERVAN

WestBow Press books may be ordered through booksellers or by contacting:

WestBow Press
A Division of Thomas Nelson & Zondervan
1663 Liberty Drive
Bloomington, IN 47403
www.westbowpress.com
844-714-3454

Scripture taken from the King James Version of the Bible.

ISBN: 978-1-6642-3031-6 (sc)
ISBN: 978-1-6642-3032-3 (hc)
ISBN: 978-1-6642-3033-0 (e)

Library of Congress Control Number: 2021907204

Print information available on the last page.

WestBow Press rev. date: 09/10/2021

To believe or not to believe is our choice, not God's demand; to bless or not to bless is God's choice, not ours to command.

---Jannie B. Johnson

Self-control or self-discipline is inner restraint—the ability to govern one's thoughts; to check one's behavior and to command one's self.

---JBJ

First, do what you should and ought; *then,* consider doing what you want and what others might be saying and doing.

---JBJ

They that wait upon the Lord shall renew their strength; they shall mount up with wings as eagles, they shall run, and not be weary; and they shall walk, and not faint. (Isaiah 40:31b (KJV)

In life, you can prepare for dying, but in death, you cannot prepare for living.

---JBJ

Table of Contents

MOTTO

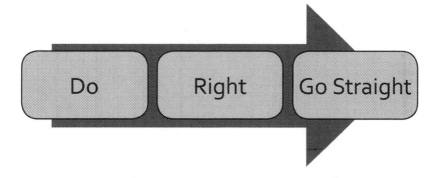

That's What It Takes.

I, Jannie Ballard Johnson believe that NO child has to be bad. I believe that youngsters can learn from others' mistakes BEFORE they make the same. They can learn how to live principle-centered lives and be happy, too. Why not? Knowing how-to live is just as important as knowing how-to make a living.

I know now that experience is NOT always the best teacher and bought sense is NOT always affordable.

A MORAL DROUGHT PRODUCES STUNTED LIVES. --JBJ

House of Representatives

The Speaker of the House and Representative Gregory L. Holloway, Sr., hereby extend their grateful appreciation and recognition to

Mrs. Jannie B. Johnson

in acknowledgment of the stalwart services she has provided to the children and families of Greater Jackson Metropolitan Area, as founder, director and teacher at the Caring n' Sharing School, which was established to teach youth the importance of avoiding mischief and becoming winners in the game of life by abiding by simple truths and principles of the Golden Rule that aid them in becoming productive citizens of society. We further recognize her outstanding humanitarianism and progressive leadership through unceasing, dedicated and merited contributions to her community with a selfless resolve to provide instruction, preventive counseling and a touch of compassion. Therefore, we hereby extend commendation and sincere appreciation for the valiant display of grace, honor and truth to those whose lives she has impacted through the Caring n' Sharing School.

*Done this the 24*th *day of June, 2018*
State Capitol
Jackson, Mississippi

Philip Gunn, Speaker
Rep. Gregory L. Holloway, Sr.
House of Representatives
House of Representatives, District 76

DEDICATION

To LEMZEL*

We prayed for you for almost ten years,
Then you came in clouds of Holy cheers.
We don't know why you took so long
But perfection takes time to grow strong.
We tried our best to do our part
To train you to be *after God's own heart.*
You blossomed through the years;
And gave no reason for regretful tears.
Now, a grown man with a wife,
Brought four lovely children to life.
Thank you for living out our dream
Fighting daily the demons unseen.
You have survived many hurtles, son.
Called to write and teach like mom.
Remember, the enemy works harder
When a champion enters his quarter.
So, Armor up and prepare for warfare;
Believe God and angels will take care.

---Mamie Crockett, April 29, 2020

Lemzel Johnson

*I am the son of Elder Lem and Jannie Johnson. I grew up with Preventive Counseling. My belief system was formed in *truth*. My behavior was developed in the "Do right, go straight" philosophy of my maternal grandfather, Herb Dr. Seth Ballard. Now, as an adult, I work with needy and deserving youth. I draw on my inner strength with confidence because I was pre-armed with *truth* and pre-warned of the *perhaps* of life. I am now a published author and motivational speaker. I desire that boys and girls everywhere could benefit from my mother's demonstrative, illustrative counseling and teaching. I did. --Lemzel B. Johnson

ACKNOWLEDGEMENTS

The author would like to thank Lauren Scott for reading the entire first draft of this book while chapters were still being researched and formatted. Then, she gave helpful suggestions that made literary sense. We also appreciate Jannie Johnson, the main character, who asked me to write her story then provided many of her written documents to form content for the story and guided me through the tweaking process.

Special gratitude is extended to my husband, Dr. Walter L. Crockett, whose patience and support allowed the sacrificed time necessary to engage in this writing project. Also, his periodic suggestions and editorial thoroughness were incredibly helpful.

Then, above all, I thank God for His wisdom and guidance through the early morning revelations when He refined ideas and revealed stories that I should include in the book. If there is anything helpful, memorable or enjoyable during or after reading this book, it's because He divinely guided me in relating the life journey of Jannie Ballard Johnson.

INTRODUCTION

Many birthdays ago, before leaving home, she was Jannie Ballard, the fourth child, and the second daughter among eight children born to Seth and Lucile Ballard. Growing up, Jannie recalls that they had few luxuries and sometimes lacked necessities, but that didn't make them "poor." Their mother and father cared for them, had faith in God and taught them to *do right and go straight,* regardless! That principle was and still is one Jannie lives by and teaches to youngsters today.

Jannie was named after her paternal grandmother, Janie McLaurin Ballard, a tall, medium sized, good-looking woman with attractive, shapely legs. Like her grandmother, she is also the fourth child in her family. Jannie's grandmother was named after her mother Janie, and Jannie is named after them all, except for the additional "n" in JAN-NIE, but, by choice, pronounced the same.

Jannie's father, Seth, was like his father, Nelson Ballard, a strong man of prayer and faith. Her paternal grandparents were also visionaries. They envisioned education for their children that wasn't foreseeable in their day. Therefore, the Ballards were considered to be community stakeholders.

Seth and Lucile's eight children—four girls and four boys-- were born at home with the assistance of a mid-wife, Bertha Parker, in the old family house off Coker Road in Pocahontas, MS. Fortunately, the children were born healthy with no mental or physical disabilities. They were fortunate and blessed to have a father with some medical understandings because there were no direct services for sickly or unhealthy African Americans during this time. Therefore, Seth Ballard provided herbal remedies for general illnesses as the family and community doctor.

Jannie's parents encouraged their children to love God, to get an education, to marry someone compatible, and to be good examples in the home and in the community. Miraculously, all the Ballard children confessed Christ at an early age and acquired scholarships to complete college with little or no expense to parents. Furthermore, five of the eight children received advanced degrees including the Ph.D. All married compatible mates and reared families without the *surgery* of divorce. The couples had reputations of being godly, wholesome family leaders in the home and in the community. The Ballards' teachings had prevailed and dreams had come true. Therefore, Jannie has endeavored to teach others those lifestyle principles for living that worked for her and her family.

The Story

To develop the story, interviews of several relatives were conducted to provide more incidences that included relationships with family members and neighbors. Her philosophy and journey embody the DNA of her forefathers and parents who fought the vestiges of slavery and inequality of civil rights. Jannie inherited the tenacity they used to be strong while rearing a family in a segregated environment.

To get a historical perspective, research was conducted on the operation of schools and the Jim Crow laws that governed the schools that Jannie attended. Her personal story incorporates a humble birth, early childhood, elementary education, parental beliefs and influences, family life and struggles.

The culmination of all these influences created the person, the wife, the mother and teacher that Jannie is today at the Caring n' Sharing School of Preventive Counseling in Madison, Mississippi. She lives by her dad's "golden rule" and uses it to teach other children the *do right and go straight* principle-centered lifestyle.

As author and Jannie's youngest sister, it was refreshing to remember and record details in Jannie's story that she had forgotten or didn't care to recall. I contemplated how best to compile and write Jannie's "biographical memoir." So, recalling what she usually says at the end of her many speeches: "I never finish talking. I just stop," I decided to allow her to narrate her own story.

Now, go ahead and read about this *seasoned* teacher. Learn. Enjoy the *Story and Teachings of Jannie Johnson*!

Mamie Ballard- Crockett, PhD

-1-

The Forming of Jannie Johnson

Before I formed thee in the belly, I knew thee; and before
thou camest forth out of the womb, I sanctified thee,
and I ordained thee a prophet unto the nations.
—Jeremiah 1:5 (KJV)

I understand that it was a cold winter's night on February 5th when I was born—the fourth of eight children. The midwife, Bertha Parker, was nodding in a chair at the foot of Momma's bed. Grandma Mary Palmer had also been told the time had come, so she was heating water in the kitchen. She always came at the birth of a new baby and stayed a few weeks until my mom got on her feet. Dad managed the older three, seeing that the older two got to Spring Hill Elementary school while Monroe, age two, stayed home.

My entrance to the world was just a few moments away. I arrived quietly only for a few seconds before the necessary spank. I cried loudly and long. And the records indicate that I never stopped making noise.

Momma and all present said I was beautiful! I inherited the light-brown/bronze Native American skin of my half Choctaw maternal grandmother with straight, dark-brown hair. Relatives said I was a pretty baby and that was why everyone wanted to hold and *kiss me*. That was somehow translated to the nickname Kisser.

Having a nickname like Kisser wasn't always fun. No kid wanted to be picked up and kissed by assorted family members, friends, or strangers. Take, for example, our neighbor Reverend Jordan.

"Hey, there she is!" said Reverend Charlie Jordan. "Come give me a kiss."

"No!" I replied as I shielded myself behind my mother and enveloped myself in her skirt.

Each time we went to chop cotton for Reverend Jordan, he would chase me around while I ran hastily to the protection of my mother's skirt. I often wondered why Momma didn't stop the harassment.

About fifty years later, I asked, "Momma, why didn't you stop Reverend Jordan?"

Momma replied matter-of-factly, "He was just playing."

But the game was not fun for me. At the time, I was only five and not quite as tall as the hoe I skillfully used to chop cotton beside my mother for two dollars a day.

The principle here is this: *If there is a game where an adult is playing with a child and the child is not having fun or is crying, parents should assess the merit of the game.* In other words, if the child is not smiling or having fun, the parent or supervising person should end the game.

Early Childhood Days

I can remember some childhood experiences as early as two-and-a-half or three. My parents said I had a bad case of being a "terrible two." I was impatient and became very upset when I didn't get my way. For instance, I would reach for something and if Momma or someone failed to give it, I would fall on the floor and roll under the bed—all the way to the wall! Momma never said how she responded or what caused me to come back from under the bed. She never spoke of the behavior as something to punish or correct. She just allowed me to stay until I cooled off. I was just being me—"temper-tantrum Kisser," she said.

However, I always liked rightness, doing right, and being fair. Whenever "right" didn't happen, I pointed it out. I also hated trouble, being silly or foolish, and looking unintelligent. I don't think this was a coincidence. I really think God designed me in my mother's womb to speak to this generation.

My dad, Seth, was also a practicing Christian. He *showed* me Christianity even though sometimes he was a little hard on me. My father fit into the traditional male roles in our household, while our mother fell into the traditional female roles. Dad was the provider and moral "barometer" who laid down the biblical principles we would live by as a family.

Childhood Experiences

I have some fond memories from my childhood. I still remember the melodious, seasoned voice of Janie McLaurin Ballard, my paternal grandmother. I was four or five years old when I first heard the songs of Bishop Charles Price Jones. The song that stayed with me throughout childhood and even today is "All I Need" in *His Fullness* songbook. The emotional and spiritual memories remain even when I sing it now. As a child, I learned the words of the chorus. "Wisdom, righteousness and power, Holiness for evermore; My redemption full and sure, He is all I need."

I didn't understand the words, but I remember and liked the way it made me feel when she sang it. The words seemed to make Big Momma feel good. And she would talk about Bishop Jones as if he were somebody supernatural. He was a young minister in the gospel who started the Holiness Movement in 1896 following the Reconstruction Years (1866–1877). The bishop was admired and cherished as a Christian trailblazer among African American people.

In my child's mind, Bishop Jones must have been a man who spoke with words of fire. I felt my grandmother's "Oo—oo" and "Aha." "My, my, my, my Lord!" I didn't get to know Bishop Jones personally, but I admired him vicariously through Big Momma's admiration for him.

In late childhood, I was still temperamental and sensitive. I always cared deeply and believed quickly. I was glad I had good people around me who positively influenced me. Nevertheless, I had to be selective about the folks I chose to believe and heed.

I didn't know my great-great-aunt Elmira Ballard Castilla (1864–1939), who was Big Momma's (Janie's) sister-in-law. But some say I have her temperament. She shared her faith also during this post slavery period when Holiness was new among African Americans.

The African Americans still experienced cruelty and social injustices from former slave masters and whites in general. Law was never on the side of former slaves, right or wrong. Therefore, prayer and a personal relationship with God became the only solace—the only constant and the real freedom.

Momma and Dad were parents with a philosophy before their time in terms of other African American parents living in a segregated society with unfair treatments and underserved educational provisions in general. Dad always said, "Cotton, the only cash crop today, will go out of business one day, but education will last."

I didn't particularly like Dad's alternative for making a living. I didn't feel good about washing herb roots. But selling herbs and seasonal vegetables on the streets of Jackson was how he acquired our basic income of at least $10 a weekend.

Even with little money, Momma would teach us using day-to-day parenting opportunities—building respect for honesty, integrity, and truth. For example, she said, "If you borrow something, give it back when you said you would. This is also true for family members. Don't ask to borrow something when you really mean 'Give me.'"

Dad was different and looked different on purpose. He wore a rope of bundled sassafras roots over his shoulder and sometimes draped the herbs over a black Dutch suit with wooden clod shoes. He had a list of herbs that treated a corresponding list of diseases and illnesses. This was his job, maybe two educated steps from what some in today's terms call home remedies.

When school started, we attended. The first days were good because in the 1950s my siblings and I were the majority present. However, when the others came after working their cotton crops, trouble started. The children would call to us, "Hey, sassafras kids! How's y'all doing?" As if they really wanted to know.

On our mile walk home after school, some schoolmates threw clods of dirt at us as we walked ahead of the crowd. Dad told us to walk ahead of the crowd because he thought that would reduce the opportunity for harassment. It didn't work. It seems that we were now perfect targets.

I really wanted to hit those bullies back. I remember the choices I made to stay out of trouble. And I remember my reasons and reasoning with myself. There was something within me that made me willing to endure the harassment, the occasional ridicule, the not-being-chosen for something, and other awful, odd feelings.

We didn't have much of a social life or friends outside of siblings. We played with each other more than with neighbors or schoolmates. The premise was that our parents didn't want us to be like the children who made fun of us. Dad predicted that they would not turn out well.

I was sensitive, but no matter how I felt, I never wanted to be a bully, loser, or pushover or feel guilty for doing something wrong. Period. That special something held the reins in my life. I know now it was someone bigger than I.

Dad was right again. Twenty years later, we found out that most of those who harassed us did not turn out so well. Dad's principle of *doing right* proved to be worthy to emulate.

Harassment Was Different from Racial Discrimination

I grew up in this south Madison County community in the late 1940s and '50s, when segregation was clearly defined by separatism and injustices. I didn't interpret those experiences in the two-tier society, African American and White, as a positive childhood experience.

After my granddad Nelson's community school closed in 1950, a new three-room building was built about one mile away from our home. We walked the distance, and some students walked even farther. There were no school buses to transport us, no utilities for our comfort, and no indoor toilets—just a new building. This was the county's demonstration of "separate but equal" enforcement of the law.

This was unfair. Students from preprimer (age five) through eighth grade (age thirteen) walked a hot, dusty road on dry days and a muddy road on rainy days because there was no gravel or pavement where African Americans lived or went to school.

Jannie at age thirteen.

Over the years, I can remember my dad's saying: *Fair laws are not automatic; they are made and maintained by good people.*

Our parents had to teach us how to survive in a hostile environment, twenty-four/seven. We were wired to think, believe and behave in an inferior manner to avoid conflict with the law. For years, I was unhappy, angry and bitter, too. I did not wish goodwill for my oppressors or the descendants of my oppressors. I wanted to get revenge! But God within me aborted that desire.

I think the most difficult decision I have had to make since trusting Jesus Christ as my Savior, was my decision to give up racial prejudice and the need to get revenge. That was NOT easy for me because I knew directly and indirectly the injustices I and my people suffered were because of race.

However, I did not want to be a hypocrite, lying to myself. So, I asked God to create in me a forgiving heart and renew the right spirit within me – the spirit of love. He gave me His kind of love and the capacity to love everybody, regardless.

If we really want some racial healing, we will have to start with self and tell the truth on ourselves first! To help others to heal, we have to be in peace to speak peace to those who still feel pain or feel guilty about the racial unrest.

It's the spirit of God's love that heals the pain and the guilt of racism and fixes the matters of the heart for both the descendants of the oppressors and the descendants of the oppressed. So, I don't get distracted by the removal of the Confederate flag (i.e., Mississippi, June 28, 2020); making new laws and policies; re-writing of history or removal of statues and monuments from public places. Most of these actions followed protests in response to the tragic death of George Floyd and others at the hands of policemen. All of these actions can and might change outward behavior, for a while. But, none of these has the power to change the matters of the heart. Kindness, forgiveness and mutual respect are behaviors generated by God--one's inner compass. After the inner readiness has matured, the necessary policies, actions, and laws will follow that will satisfy the masses.

- 2 -

My Parents

Looking back at history can make seeing
ahead clearer. --Jannie Johnson

Before I was born and went to Spring Hill Elementary school, there
were my parents. I want to introduce them to you in a special way
and then introduce you to their parents. I could leave some parts
out, but I enjoyed the stories and I hope my readers will tolerate the
details. You see, some African-American families have difficulty
finding family roots because many times the family trees were
cut off; severed at the base. Stumps were left, but slavery would
grind family members into tiny pieces like a stump grinder, leaving
fragmented families.

Therefore, here is the story of how my mother and father
met and how they overcame many challenges. They experienced
blessings along the way, and they found a method to ameliorate
life's madness.

The relationship began when my dad, Seth, went to a church
social at Christian Union Church in Madison. He was looking for
a prospective wife, a young lady to marry and start a family. At
the social, he met some very attractive Palmer girls who were also
looking for good Christian men.

Seth Ballard, A 1924 graduate of Alcorn Agricultural College

Lucile Palmer was one of nine one-fourth-Native-American children of Mary and Allen Palmer. All the children were light skinned with dark wavy hair. At first sight Seth was attracted to her. He said he wanted his children to have lighter skin than his because it would help them progress faster in the post slavery era. During this time, he was convinced that the light-skinned African Americans received favor from the Whites and from other African-American people, too. So, he wanted to marry one of these attractive girls.

Lucile Palmer Ballard, My Mother

At home in Madison, Lucile's mother had made it very difficult to live there. Therefore, Lucile, now twenty-two years old, was ready to marry. "I just want a good man!" she pondered.

Her mother Mary, being a child of a slave, saw severe whipping of slaves early in life and thought that was the way to rear children. That's why she kept a switch for each of her nine children over her porch so she could whip them periodically "to keep them good," she explained.

One day after a painful whipping, Lucile looked out of her bedroom window and saw a full moon just over the trees. She prayed, "Moon, when you go down, tell God, to send me a husband; someone to take care of me, and love me."

At this church social, God answered her prayer. Courtship was not a long process in those days. Seth and Lucile were married within a year after the social at Christian Union Church in 1933.

My dad, Seth, now in his early thirties and a newlywed, still felt the responsibility of helping his mother pay the $220 loan payment for the land plus taxes on the 182 acres of land.

Seth quieted his thoughts with prayer. Later on, when confronted with a business situation, he just trusted God to give him peace and comfort, and increase his faith.

Almost immediately, a 103-year-old former slave came riding by on a horse. (We never knew his name, so we refer to him as "Mr. Ex.") He stopped and asked Dad his name and if he had attended school. Dad told him he had attended grammar school in Madison County and high school and college at Christ Missionary Industrial College and studied the trade of Painting at Alcorn College.

"I think you would make a good Herb Doctor." "Mr. Ex" responded encouragingly.

"Herb Doctor? What is that?" Dad inquired.

"I'd like to show you the herbs that grow on Mississippi lands and in woods. I'll teach you how to identify each herb through at least four senses: seeing, touching, smelling, tasting as well as the likely location.

"Mr. Ex" further explained that every region naturally grows herbs needed to heal diseases of the people who live in that region.

I sure hope you will commit to keeping this herbal practice going. Don't let it die; our people need it." Mr. EX pleaded.

Over the following weeks, Seth received hands-on experience in herbal medicines from the Mr. Ex who became his mentor. He learned how to use roots, barks, leaves, cores, stems, and flowers from trees, bushes, vines, and various grasses and weeds to make nature's medicines into teas, potions, tonics, and salves.

My dad's most popular tea was Sassafras. It had many benefits for a people with little or no access to medical services. The fresh or dried bark of the root was boiled until the water turned a reddish brown. It was effective as a stimulant to flush out the kidneys. It has an agreeable spicy odor that was known to help clear skin conditions including varicose vein ulcers, inflamed eyes, rheumatism, gout and syphilitic infections.

Nevertheless, my dad, Seth Ballard, became our family doctor and served many other families in the Pocahontas, MS community with several herbs that cured common childhood illnesses and diseases. No immunization shots were offered in our community, and a few were available nationwide.

In 1950, Dad was featured in the Ebony Magazine as the best Herb Doctor in the region. That publicity generated more out of state clients. He built a one-room office in the backyard to better serve the increased clientele. Dad was to us a famous man, yet a balanced person.

To make this point, he believed in his civic duty of voting when African- Americans weren't allowed to vote under normal circumstances. When African-American people voted, they had to pay poll taxes or answer questions like, "How many bubbles are in a bar of soap?" Many were not able to pay poll taxes or answer unreasonable questions. But my dad thought it was worth the sacrifice.

When asked how he managed to vote when many other African Americans did not, he said, "I mumbled words and acted like I didn't know what I was doing. I shuffled my feet slowly with my head tilted downward and said with a condescending whine: That white man over yonder told me I could come up here and vote."

The pollster, would look up in dismay and respond, "Here, take the ballot, boy. Go over to that back table and check off who you are voting for. Oh, can you read, boy?"

"Yes 'um."

During those days, Dad also said that African Americans had to step off the sidewalk if a white person was approaching him or her going in opposite direction. This, of course, was one of several injustices during the early 1900s. The family has a copy of a letter my dad wrote to Frederick Douglas to see how they could work together to make things better for African Americans. Conditions were much better than slavery, but far from what was equal, fair and just.

These were turbulent times, but my dad stood firm with the cause. On June 11, 1963, President Kennedy made a strong statement on the immediate need for civil rights legislation (John F. Kennedy Library, TNC:262). He said in the videoed *Address to the Nation* that: "The [African-American] baby born in America today ... has about one-half as much chance of completing high school as a white baby born in the same place on the same day; one-third as much chance of completing college; one third as much chance of becoming a professional man; twice as much chance of becoming unemployed ... ; a life expectancy that is seven years less, and the prospects of earning only half as much" [in salaries].

During this time, I was not in Mississippi, but I was still a part of the racial situations among African Americans everywhere. My dad, Herb Doctor Seth Ballard, collaborated with Medgar Evers and Martin Luther King in preparation for the March on Washington in which he later participated (August 1963). After the June 1963 assassination of Medgar Evers, President Kennedy wanted to initiate a process to end the unfair labor practices in Federal establishments that were not hiring a diverse population, especially no African Americans. My dad encouraged 19-year-old daughter, Mamie—a college student, to accept the offer President Jacob L. Reddix of Jackson State College had made to anyone willing to integrate a Federal building in Jackson, MS. Integrating federal establishments was a civil rights policy mandated by President John

F. Kennedy. Prior to this, no African Americans held positions in the Internal Revenue Office, Social Security or any other federal businesses in Mississippi except for the postal service. Even there, no Postmaster positions were occupied by African Americans in 1963. This mandate occurred in response to the racial unrest across the country especially in Mississippi following the tragic death of Medgar Evers that occurred two weeks earlier in June 1963.

The civil rights bill would end segregation as we had known it. For I did not know or understand racial discrimination. It was not explained. It had been my experience all of my life for generations. But I had no living ex-slave relatives, no free African Americans alive who could tell me how slavery was different from limited freedom with pronounced racial discrimination in America. I just knew, based on oral history, that what I have now is better than slavery, but less than equal justice and civil rights.

As mentioned earlier, my dad participated in the March on Washington where Martin Luther King delivered the memorable speech, *I Have a Dream*. In the fall of 1963, President Kennedy was assassinated and Vice President Lyndon B. Johnson assumed the presidency and felt compelled to complete what President Kennedy had started in terms of civil rights, voting rights and justice for all people.

In l964, the Civil Rights Bill was passed. Most important of all, the Civil Rights bill that Kennedy had proposed before his death in 1963 was even a stronger bill after his tragic death. President Johnson said it was his first, and maybe only, opportunity to ensure the bill was broad and written properly to reduce discrimination. It was.

The package gave the attorney general of the United States the power to sue southern state governments that operated segregated schools. It included a strong provision giving African Americans equal access to public transportation and accommodations. African Americans could now go to any restaurants, lounges, hotels, and motels. We, African Americans, could choose to go to any public school, college or university. We could apply for work at any federal business or agency. The bill would cut off any federally sponsored programs or businesses that discriminated based on race.

Now, it was time for African Americans to understand their rights and the new privileges as citizens when facing possible White opposition. Whites and African Americans from the north worked with southern leaders to establish Freedom Summer Schools. This was like summer school for developing race relations. Their job was to meet with rural and urban community leaders and get them to invite local people and church groups to the community meetings.

At that time, I was still off in school, but I knew my dad was a local leader and would be involved in the movement. Even though I was a young adult, my childhood fears surfaced again. I was afraid for the life and safety of my dad. Feeling hopeless, I just cried and prayed, prayed and cried, having no recourse.

With unified courage, my parents initially housed two White female college students, and later a young white male. Before coming, they were specially trained for civil rights work somewhere in Ohio. They learned of the possible confrontations with the Jim Crow laws in the south and the ultimate danger involved. They were specifically taught about the challenges of voter registration and how to conduct themselves if attacked. In Mississippi, role playing and demonstrations were presented and taught in the local churches that conducted the Freedom Summer School of 1964.

However, the three Civil Rights workers (Michael Schwerner, Andrew Goodman of Arizona and James Chaney of Mississippi) did not escape the violent hands of the Ku Klux Klan during this time. The three had worked together to help organize voter registration efforts on behalf of the Congress of Racial Equality (CORE). The workers were followed to a remote area of Philadelphia, MS where they were working. The Klan members shot them and buried them in a mound of dirt at a construction site.

Therefore, my parents were very concerned about safety of the visiting civil rights workers in our community, especially those who lived in our home. To ensure safety, my father said he sat on our screened in porch and guarded our premises during the night. He shot the gun off periodically to deter troublemakers who usually came around at night to plant a bomb or set the dwelling on fire. Our home was a target because we housed civil rights workers.

However, the summer ended peacefully in the Ballards' quarters. In gratitude, the civil rights workers pitched in to remodel the Ballards' porch—restructuring it with a concrete foundation. Community service was heartfelt on both sides.

In the summer of 1965, the Voting Rights Bill was passed. That fall of 1965, the NAACP asked my dad to help identify a few young African-American children in elementary school who would integrate the white schools in Flora, MS. My first cousin, Sweet Wiggins, and her cousin, Sue Porter, were asked to accept the challenge. Sweet was in second grade, and Sue was in third. Again, my dad was available to guide and support them in this brave venture.

These are just a few of the events that occurred during my early life and college years. These Civil Rights events punctuated the life of my father, Seth Ballard (1897--1973) and my mother, Lucile Palmer Ballard (1911--1996) who stood with him.

Family Fears During the Struggle for Civil Rights

Through the years, my dad's life was threatened several times before the passing of the Civil Rights and Voting Rights Bills that caused the desegregation of schools, public facilities, transportation and other services.

I remember the time Dad had to get out of Mississippi for about three months because of racial issues. Momma had to care for eight children alone during that period. After that experience, I used to cry each time he went into town to sell his herbs and goods. I was afraid he might go away and stay. Other times, I feared someone would kill him because of his Civil Rights involvement. Now, as an adult, I cried silently at the thought of such a tragedy.

Why did he do this against the odds when it was not politically correct, during the 40s, 50s and early 60s? It was not popular for an African-American man to be focused and purpose-driven? His civil rights actions caused him to receive racial slurs from some.

They were neither complimentary nor encouraging. Yet, he took the risk for the greater good on behalf of family and community. The Ballard children and others of their generation benefitted from sacrifices made by dad and other civic minded citizens. They wanted for us what they did not have--a better life, full citizenship in this rich and prosperous United States of America.

Historically, my father was the last of the practicing Herb Doctors in Mississippi. He was an advocate for the family, for good health, for social justice, for civil rights and for educational equality.

Herb Doctor Seth Ballard, was a purpose-driven man. The kind of father he chose to be and the type of man he dared to model in his home and in his community were characteristics of strength and vision. The neighbors respected him and some loved him too. They looked out for him by reporting to him any rumors of danger planned for him. Thankfully, none of the threats materialized. He died of natural causes in 1973.

The Ballard Siblings (1989)
Left to right: Samuel, Sylvester, Mamie, Monroe,
Daisy, Rosie Mae, Seth, Jr. and Jannie

However, most of us were married with a family by the time our father passed. But we learned a lot before we left home.

For example, I learned from my parents that prayer is a powerful tool. When situations seemed totally impossible, like sending eight children to college, my parents held fast, prayed and believed.

The Ballard children went to college and beyond and our parents never paid for tuition, clothes or books. We all received scholarships of various kind that met our scholastic needs. I praise God for the spiritual leadership of my father and the close spiritual followship of my mother. But through it all, my father proved to be the real hero.

A Tribute to My Father, Seth Ballard

My father, Seth
My father *was* great
He wasn't just an ordinary man!
He had a spirit-controlled mind that made him kind.
He had a religion that was worth his time.
He worshipped a God he called mine.
He had eight children and never complained.
"Oh well," he said, "My Father is rich in houses and land."
"I want my children to go to school—Lord, what shall I do?"
"Follow Me, my son, I will see them through."
Father had no money; life got rough; it wasn't funny.
My great father didn't lose his nerve.
He had a Super Father up above.
Many times, we had recycled clothes and no-good shoes on our feet.
"Don't' worry, you children, as long as you have food to eat."
We went to school, sat in our seats, where no other eyes we did meet.
There we were the blessed few whom the Lord said, "I'll see through."
My great father had convictions: he knew right and wrong weren't a mixture.
My great father made a name; throughout the nation people read of his fame.
Closer home, they called him "Doc."
That served him right. He was a super MAN and nobody's flop! --Jannie Johnson,

- 3 -

My Maternal DNA

Dream big! You are never too young or
too old to pursue your dream.
--Jannie B. Johnson, Cn'S School

Education was and still is a part of my DNA, but the strong moral
side came through the holiness church teachings as well as from
my mother, Lucile, and grandmother, Mary Nash Palmer. But I'm
not born yet. Let me tell you some oral history about my maternal
grandmother, Mary Nash Palmer. I have a few moral seeds thrown
in from her as well as from her temperament.

Mary was one of two daughters of Mariah ("Emily") Nash, a
slave. Her father was recorded as John Nash, a full-blooded Native
American. Her sister, Lucy, had a different father, a dark African-
American man.

Emily (one-half Native American herself), worked for a
Choctaw Native American family. A young male of the family
befriended her saying that white men don't treat pretty women
right. And, convincingly said that Native Americans treat their
women better. She believed him. Their relationship became
intimate. She became pregnant with Mary, my grandmother. He
not only proved to be untrustworthy, he was also mean. As a result,
Emily's personality also grew meaner and bitter. Therefore, she
taught her girls to be chaste and virtuous.

She instructed, "Don't trust men! Don't let them touch you! If one says he loves you, make sure he has something to give you and plans to take care of you." Then, she added, "After you are sure he cares about you and you also love him, then marry him. Have no children before you marry! You hear me?"

Then, many times, great grandma Emily's instructions would be punctuated with a whipping for each of her girls. "This," she said, "is to make sure they are listening." Mary, the oldest girl, learned to listen well.

When her daughter, Mary Nash became a teenager, she married Allen Palmer, the son of Amelia (three-fourth Native American) and Julius Palmer, an African-American dark-skinned slave.

The story is that Amelia had light complexion with long straight dark hair. She and her five sisters and brothers had been sold to a nearby plantation in about 1850. In her new location, Amelia was admired from across the field by Julius Palmer. Julius Palmer, a dark-skinned man, asked his master to buy Amelia for him. The slave master bought Amelia for Julius. Amelia and Julius Palmer had an instant attraction for each other and developed a romantic relationship. They soon married and to this union, nine children were born. The names of their nine adult children are listed here with spouses, if any, and the others are listed singly: Ollie Palmer (Estelle), Alfred Palmer (Bessie), Otis Palmer, Audra Palmer, Ella Palmer (Julius Bass), Rosie Palmer and James Palmer. James was married, but I'm not sure of his wife's name. He, however, settled in the Memphis area. And, the youngest, Allen Palmer (my grandfather) married Mary Nash (my grandmother) and they lived on their own land.

To Allen and Mary Palmer were born eight very light skinned children with dark wavy hair. The Palmers all were hard workers and cared for their land. The children later married and some moved away. They are listed here with their spouses: Rosie Lee (Charles Price Ballard); Lucile (Seth Ballard)—my parents; L. F. Palmer (Lillie), Ida Mae (Phillip Thompson); Benjamin Palmer (Rebecca); Earlene (Walter Cannon); Allen Palmer, Jr. (Jeannette); and Mamie (Nathan Wiggins).

However, the land ownership did not last long after the adult children moved out. Grandpa Allen Palmer's father was Julius Palmer.

He had accumulated for his family 80 acres of land in the Madison area. He gave each of his children a house seat. His son, Alfred Palmer, was the executor. One year, Alfred lacked the funds to pay the taxes for the family land. The Palmers lost the land due to unpaid taxes. A White man, Stewart ("Steve") Hoy, bought the land for almost nothing.

This was another experience that was common to African-American families--losing their family's land due to the lack of tax payments or trickery. On one hand, there was no recourse for the Palmers, no due process or laws to support African-Americans at that time. On the other hand, White families had the connections and the where-with-all to claim or reclaim property for the sum of taxes due.

Nevertheless, Allen and Mary Palmer with a few of their adult children remained on the previously owned family land as sharecroppers.

Years later, the Lewis Callie family bought the land from Mr. Steve Hoy. Allen and Mary Palmer became the caregivers of Lewis Callie's children (Luke and Bethie). The Callies told the Palmers they could stay on the land, cost free, as long as they wanted, even until death.

Mary was the primary caregiver for the Callies' children until they became adults. As promised, the Callies gave Grandpa Allen and Grandma Mary permission to stay, cost free, on the land. That was a real blessing for this elderly couple.

In 2020, the former Palmer land located near Bennet Chapel in Madison is where the remains of the Palmer ancestors have been relocated. Some poorly marked graves were dismantled during the construction of a predominately White subdivision developed in the 1980s.

Over the years, I heard this story and other stories like our family's. I witnessed the last part of my grandparents' story. Their experience helped me understand how easy it is to lose one's inheritance, never to be regained.

These vicarious and personal experiences caused me to value, even more, family, family land and the Madison homeplace where I now conduct the Caring n' Sharing School that was originally built by my paternal grandfather.

Emily Bradford Nash was not a loving mother to my grandmother, Mary Nash Palmer. In fact, she was so mean that Grandma Mary chose to live with her grandmother—a freed slave. (I don't recall her name, but Aunt Mamie Wiggins thinks her last name was Williams.)

The story is that my great grandmother never forgave the Native Indian who enticed her into a relationship. As a result of this bad experience that produced a child (Mary), she many times took her frustrations out on Grandma Mary, whipping her severely--sometimes without an explanation.

When Grandma Mary was older, Great Grandmother Emily warned her about "certain" men and how to behave. Grandma Mary taught and warned her girls the same way when she had her girls. My mother, Lucile, was one of them. This could be the genesis for my determination to teach chastity and purity to our youth today.

I confess that, other than personal salvation, I don't know all that caused me and my siblings to adhere to high moral standards. However, I think Grandma Mary influenced us in one way or another.

Grandma Mary Palmer (1880--1986)

To grandma Mary, I say: "Your influence is now five generations strong. Most of the females are holding on to your biblical (or enticed) moral standards." The results freed us to be children when we were children, and to be chaste until we were married.

My parents and grandparents were married before having children. That was important to them. It also became a moral standard for the Lucile and Seth Ballard's children.

I remember my standards were tested when I went to live with Aunt Bessie. I dated for a short time Clyde Brandon. At the end of the date, he parked the car near our house and started scooting under me. I asked, "What are you doing?" He said, "You know what I'm doing!"

"Well, if you are trying to do what I think, the answer is NO!" I said emphatically.

"Well then, this is not going to work out between you and me." Brandon responded.

I said, "fine!" Then, went into the house and slammed the door.

Shortly thereafter, I heard Clyde Brandon was getting married and the girl was already pregnant.

"Oh, I'm glad I had the inner strength to say NO." I confessed to myself.

While Growing up, Grandma Mary Didn't like Me

"That gal is too feisty," said Grandma Mary. I was around age twelve when I heard Grandma Mary say, "I'm going to put an X in Kisser's back right now. She ain't gonna 'mount to nothing. Mark my words."

"I'm going to disprove you!" I thought to myself with determination. I never knew why Grandma Mary had such low expectations of me except she was kind of temperamental and outspoken. (That sounds like what people said about me.)

My appearance also got attention because I now had sandy wavy hair and my complexion was still a few shades lighter than most of my siblings. Some neighbors used to even tease my dad of possible infidelity in the family since he was a dark-skinned man with "tightly curled hair." They questioned his fatherhood with their eyes. However, few questioned my legitimacy when they saw my light -skinned mother with shoulder-length hair.

Nevertheless, my dad, Seth, seemed to struggle with the implications of his neighbors. He began to be a little impatient with me whenever I had concerns. Other times he would give me more chores to complete and fuss at me if I complained. His famous words were, "Girl, pick up your lips!" He was insinuating that I should stop pouting. Sometimes my siblings would come to my rescue and help me with the extra chores.

One of the chores was washing his various herb roots and twigs. I didn't like washing the herbal roots. Even though herbs were our regular medicine, I only help wash the roots when I had to or was assigned extra duty for unruly behavior.

- 4 -

My Paternal DNA

Life does not choose right or wrong, people
do. --Caring n' Sharing School

The history of my forefathers may help to unpack how I became a person of strong-will and determination. It is on the foundational strength of their moral and spiritual shoulders that I now stand. Therefore, I want to share their journey that innately propelled me to serve my community from the one-room school building that now houses the Caring n' Sharing School.

My Grandpa Nelson and Grandma Janie married and moved their family into an old mansion house that once belonged to "the boss." In those days, the boss (usually a white slave owner) lived in the big house and the slaves, or the later sharecroppers, lived in the smaller houses nearby.

In the big house, several of their nine children were born. The couple was very ambitious and wanted to get a "toe hold" by the time their children were school age. They heard of a land sale. They went and looked at the land for sale, liked it and decided to buy it in 1904. Even though it was about twenty miles from Jackson, Grandpa Nelson and Janie Ballard were not discouraged because they now owned property.

Several years later, tragedy hit the young family. The oldest child, Essell James, was crushed under the wheels of a rolling wagon. He later died of those injuries at about age twenty. This was heart-breaking, but it didn't deter them from the immediate desire to build a school for their children and others in the community.

Their second child, Seth, was different in that he read a lot and spent time meditating. However, it was Seth who kept the family going after his father Nelson left home suddenly because of a racial confrontation.

It was not wise during this time, to argue or disagree with a white man. But being a proud resourceful man, my grandfather stood his ground. An argument started with a neighbor, Mr. West, who objected to Nelson's putting a fence on his newly acquired property that would inconvenience him when he would travel around or walk in the neighborhood. Mr. West complained that the fence would eliminate his convenient shortcut.

Mr. West gave him a lot of trouble and many others joined with him against Granddaddy Nelson because they had similar problems with the fence. Granddaddy told Mr. West, a white man, not to cross his property anymore and he was proceeding to put up a fence around his property. Mr. West ignored his request and continued riding through the property as big as ever. This situation and emotions mounted beyond conversation. Granddaddy threatened Mr. West.

Nelson felt certain there would be further trouble, so he talked it over with wife Janie and they both decided that Nelson needed some time away until things cooled down. Nelson decided to stay with his brother in Greenville, Mississippi and work there in an ice plant to help support his family.

While in Greenville, my Granddaddy Nelson became very ill. Being afraid and not eating properly he developed what we know now as colon cancer. He died of "acute indigestion" at age forty-three. Family and friends heard of my Granddad Nelson's death and offered support to my Grandma Janie and her children. The Ballards were admired as pillars of this little community. Everyone knew them for establishing a place of worship (Ballard Chapel) that was also their school building (Spring Hill Elementary) during the week (c.1917--50).

These tragic experiences didn't break the family, but kept

them grounded. God was faithful. My dad, Seth, and his siblings (Janie, Percy Max, Bessie, Celeste Theresa, Charles Price, and Victor Sylvester) supported their mother. They all attended Spring Hill Elementary school and high school at Christ Missionary and Industrial College in Jackson. All finished high school during a time when most African Americans were not allowed to go to public schools.

Grandma Janie lived by faith—one day at a time.   I learned that trials and hard times can make a person bitter or better. She chose to be better.

Due to remodeling over the years, the original schoolhouse is not visible from the exterior. The horizonal rooms behind the screened porch constitute the original one-room school that expanded to a two-room school built by Nelson and Janie Ballard with support from neighbors. The pitched roof with chimneys on each end is the actual school building and the chimneys replaced the doors on each end. This school met a dire need during the early 1900s when there were no schools in the Madison, Mississippi area for African Americans.

The School House Became Family Home
(1952) after family home burned.
It now houses the Caring n' Sharing School (1994--)

My dad maintained the property and kept the family farm going. He had attended Alcorn Agricultural College (the first land grant college) where he learned how to farm and how to paint houses. Later, he learned about the herbal medicines and committed to the practice to maintain his family's health and that of the community people in the greater Jackson area from the 1930s to early 1960s.

In addition to the medical service to his community, Dad leased land to neighbors who needed more farm land to raise cotton. My dad maintained a truck farm so that his children would have food, but would not have to stay out of school during cotton-picking seasons.

To supplement his herbal income, he made molasses for the community. Farmers brought bundles of sugar cane to Dad to extract the juices to make molasses. He would grind stalks of sorghum or sugar cane with his mill propelled by a mule-pulled crane. This raw cane juice was then cooked in a special pan for hours before producing fresh molasses for family and neighbors.

The Truck Farm and the Bicycle Ride that Helped My Self-Esteem

I worked better in the fields—chopping other folks' cotton or plowing in our family truck farm. When Momma and I used to work in the fields, I earned extra money from the neighbors who raised cotton. We had a "truck" farm wherein we raised everything except cotton. While my physical self-image was positive, I had to hold on to and build a healthy self-esteem by gathering evidence about what I was like as a person. One piece of evidence was my aptitude to work and find solutions.

I remember a big problem occurred on one hot summer Saturday. My parents were preparing vegetables to sell in Jackson. Everyone helped shell and pack quart bags of peas, butterbeans, okra and bundle the bunches of greens. We packed all in a bag like a Crocker sack. All was ready to be loaded on a wagon that would take my parents and the load to the community Bus Stop. Since most families did not have cars, the travel connection was designed by Mr. Payne's Grocery in Jackson to take country folks from the dusty roads of Pocahontas to the big capitol city to do business or go shopping.

My dad had on his usual khaki outfit with a string of sassafras herbs across his shoulder just in case he came across a buyer for his "herbal roots that cured most common illnesses," he always said.

"Hey, Momma, are you ready?" That's what Dad called our mother. He said it was so we little ones would learn to call her *Momma* or *Mom*. Our mother, Lucile, also called our father, *Daddy*, for the same reason.

"Yes, coming, Daddy" she replied as she gave final directions to Rosa, the oldest girl, about fourteen, who had to keep house while both were out.

Monroe, about twelve years old, was at the reins to steer the wagon down the dirt road to the Bus Stop.

"All aboard!" he shouted. "Yes, sir! They fondly responded.

"Get up!" Monroe directed the horses as they headed out. Rosa, Jannie, Daisy, Mamie and Samuel stood and waved until the wagon disappeared down the first hill about a mile from our house. Seth, Jr. the oldest was in school at Piney Woods and Sylvester was not yet born.

I spotted the bag of vegetables left on the table.

"Wow!" they left the vegetables they are supposed to sell!" I thought frantically. "I can catch them!"

I did the only thing a daring ten-year-old would do. I loaded the sack on back of Monroe's bike and rushed to catch the wagon before they got to the bus line.

I rode hard and fast, plaits tossing in the wind as my feet peddled as fast as I could over bumps and lumps in the dirt road. Up and down hills that seemed impossible to climb on a bike, she rode. My adrenaline kicked in and there was no stopping or time to get tired.

"Butterbeans and okra to sell! If I don't catch them there will be no sale! No sale, no money for food!" The thoughts raced through my young mind.

I hollered, "Momma! Dad! Monroe!" I called all of their names just in case one of them heard me. Maybe it was God who heard me because no one seemed to hear. Yet, I persevered.

The wagon was in sight! I saw it go down the next hill while I was going up. I was getting closer, but not close enough to yell and get them to stop. The hills have no mercy and there were three steep hills to climb. Just as I got to the point of going down a hill the wagon was at a point of going down the next hill. Down the hill I went at break-neck speed with power to climb up the next hill.

I was glad Monroe's bike was built for speed. This meant he installed a small sprocket on the back wheel. It was fine for speed, but I needed strength to peddle the bike up hills! My strength came miraculously. I peddled up the steep hills with my girlish strength just in time to see the wagon peek the next hill and disappear once again. Only godly strength, sheer guts and determination could energize me to climb another hill. This time the wagon was on a more level part of the road and I got within distance to holler.

Then with the little remaining breath I yelled, "Momma!"

Momma heard the little raspy squeak and turned. She saw me—a dusty, sweat-drenched Jannie waving them down. They stopped the wagon and waited. By then they realized I had the sack of vegetables they'd left. I knew my parents were elated and grateful, but my Momma only said, "Good you caught us."

I was fulfilled in knowing I had prevented a major problem. It was a sign of a healthy self-esteem, not narcissistic in an unhealthy way like thinking I was better than all others. I had self-worth, believing that I was lovable and valuable regardless of some of my faults, like pouting.

My self-esteem was enhanced. Self-esteem is also realizing one's potential and having a sense of belonging. It may have been initiated and preserved since age five when my mother said I was a good worker. Therefore, it was no problem to work beside my mother in the fields, chopping cotton—pulling a hoe that was one-third taller than I.

But I also could have questioned self-esteem if I evaluated my shaky relationship with my father. But during those times, my siblings helped me maintain a good self-esteem. I recall talking to my siblings about anything that was bothering me. That social base kept me grounded and helped build my self-esteem when I felt low in spirit.

My dad had a family meeting on Sundays after a big breakfast with homemade biscuits. Momma and Dad conducted church at home because we didn't have a car to travel to the family church at New Lake Church of Christ Holiness in Jackson, MS. Momma read the scriptures and Dad explained them. Dad majored in big things, the big picture teaching us how to live peaceful lives. He even warned us of choosing role models at church. He said learn about God from the Bible because sometimes people will disappoint you. Once he said, "Man without God will do unkind things." Dad was more of a faith person. Momma took care of the details, the process. They complemented each other.

On marriage, for example, Momma taught, 'No divorce, just iron it out. Put it all on the table." That means, *talk it out*. Spread out the issues so both sides of the situation can be seen; rather than seeing the problem within each other.

I learned that family background has a lot to do with how one sees life, how one makes decisions, and how past examples of family members can help one in handling current difficult situations.

I am glad my family stood strong and made a contribution to the community. It is because of what they did that gave me and still gives me the motivation and strength to teach in the same building they built over a hundred years ago. The Caring n' Sharing School exists and proports the same "Do Right and Go Straight" principle because they did.

- 5 -

Childhood and Beyond:
Learning to Believe

When you look at me, you see someone who
has been becoming for generations.
--Jannie Johnson

I grew up in a Christian home where I saw how parents pray when problems were too big for them to handle. However, celebrating Christmas, Santa Claus and getting Christmas presents posed a different kind of understanding. I learned that Jesus's birthday was Christmas Day, but somehow Santa Claus would be celebrated more with little or no connection to Jesus. What about this Santa Claus?

I believed in Santa Claus when I was a child. My Momma and Dad did not say there was or wasn't a Santa Claus. But my peers gave me enough reasons to believe plus I wanted to believe. Why? Because I liked the idea of Santa bringing me everything I wanted if I'd been good. I did not know or understand that there was a direct connection between my parents' budget and Santa's gift giving. I later learned the truth, and it was shockingly painful. But I am no longer a child so I gradually put away childish things.

Years ago, when I taught at The Learning Tree Child Development Center, the director, Mamie Crockett, taught the history of Santa Claus along with the true Christmas story. The story of Jesus' birth was related to the first appearance of *Santa Claus*. He was actually St. Nicholas who lived in a little town in England during the 1700s. He saw that many poor children did not get gifts at Christmas time so he purchased gifts of various kinds to place at the doors of needy children. Initially, parents didn't know where the gifts came from, but were so happy and grateful to have something for their children. Eventually, they discovered St. Nicholas, a Christian saint, was the giver who made this a part of his ministry.

If we, the Ballard children, lived during the 1700s when St. Nicholas became known world-wide, we would have been one of the special families chosen at Christmastime. We always had something in our "pans"–not stockings--on Christmas. But we usually had to share toys. For example, one doll for three girls; one wagon for three boys and no toys for the older children who received more apples, oranges and candies than the younger ones.

For us, it was an exciting time, a special time to share and play house, etc. We also received little boxes of raisins, nuts from our family orchard, corn candy, apples and oranges that we could eat whenever we wanted. However, we didn't eat all the goodies on Christmas Day because we knew these special treats would not appear until Christmas of next year. Who said we were poor? "Not I" was my thinking at the time.

Now that I am a grandmother, I have had to retell the whole scenario about Christmas. I wrote a special version of the Christmas story for my grandchildren and friends that appeared in the Clarion-Ledger (December 23, 2007) based on a historical article published in the 19th century.

Yes, Trizel, There Is a Christ of Christmas

"Please tell me the truth; is there a Santa Claus?" asked Trizel. Like in 1897, the eight-year-old Virginia O'Hanlon asked her dad, Dr. Philip O'Hanlon, whether Santa Claus really existed. The story is that Virginia had begun to doubt whether there was a Santa Claus because her friends had told her that he did not exist.

Rather than answering his daughter's question, Dr. O'Hanlon told her to write to the New York Sun, a prominent New York City newspaper at that time. He assured her that the paper would tell her the truth.

Virginia believed her dad and followed his instructions. She wrote the editor a little two-sentence letter. Her request and question were: "Please tell me the truth. Is there a Santa Claus?"

Veteran newsman Francis Pharcellus Church wrote The Sun's response to Virginia's inquiry. It appeared as an unsigned editorial on September 21, 1897.

He wrote: "Virginia, your little friends are wrong. They have been affected by the skepticism of a skeptical age. They do not believe except for what they see. They think that nothing can be which is not comprehensible by their little minds. All minds, Virginia, whether they be of men or of children, are little ...

"Yes, Virginia, there is a Santa Claus. He exists as certainly as love, generosity and devotion exist. You know that they abound and give your life its highest beauty and joy ...

Nobody Sees Santa

Nobody sees Santa Claus, but that is no sign that there is no Santa Claus. The most real things in the world are those that neither children nor man can see ..."

"No Santa Claus! Thank God he lives and he lives forever ... (He will continue to make glad the heart of childhood." The journalist concluded.

We are not living in the 19th century, but we still have little Virginias and big Virginias who are beginning to have doubts about a lot of things. They—our Virginias—have different names like Trizel, Zarya, Zavier, Lem, Jr., Whitney, Bettie Jo, Junior, Zack and others.

They have questions about Christmas, too because some of their friends, young ones and old ones, are saying that there is no Christ of Christmas. They say that saying "Merry Christmas" is not politically correct. That, instead, one should say, "Happy Holidays."

Today's Virginias need somebody to tell them the truth; is there a Christ of Christmas? They need some Mr. Churches. The names don't matter! Their names could be dad, editor, pastor, teacher, neighbor, scout master, or anybody who can remember America as one nation under God. They need folks who still value those Christian principles that made America the land that we love, the land of the free and the home of the brave.

Believing Without Seeing

Like the editor, Mr. Church, we must not cover the truth. Yes, Trizel, there is a Christ of Christmas. He is the reason for the season. Your little friends, young and old, are wrong. They have been affected by the skepticism of skeptical age. They do not believe except for what they see. No human kind can conceive or imagine all the wonders there are unseen and unsee-able in this world.

Consider the air. Take a deep breath. Blow into your hand. What do you see? Anything? I think not, but don't try to live without that unseen thing. Breathe!

Zarya, the minds of men or of children are too limited to grasp the wholeness of truth and the omniscience of the Creator. Man's intellect cannot comprehend the boundless world about him, but God admonishes us to get wisdom and understanding.

Wisdom is the principal thing; therefore, get wisdom: and with all thy getting get understanding. (Proverbs 4:7 KJV, Public Domain)

Brittney, Whitney, Zavier, be wise and believe. If you choose not to believe in the Christ of Christmas because you cannot see Him or you cannot prove His authenticity, scientifically, what does that prove? Nobody sees Christ, but that is no sign that there is no Christ. Right? However, there is overwhelming evidence that Christ lives.

Left to right: Lemzel (Junior), Zarya,
Zavier and Trizel Johnson (2015)

Bettie Jo, without the Christ of Christmas there would be no love, generosity or devotion. There would be no purpose for today and no reason to hope for tomorrow. This would be a dreary world without faith.

Is it all real? Ah-h-h, Junior, Zack, and Lem, Jr. and all you precious ones, in all the world there is nothing else more real and abiding! Thank God, the Christ of Christmas lives today and He lives forever. Like you, Santa Claus, is just another expression of life and God's love. Just breathe, my children. Inhale. Exhale ...

- 6 -

Country Life and the Plum Bush Experience

The journey of life is too long for shallow
thinking and emotional behavior.
--Jannie Johnson

Have you ever used a clothesline? In my day, that was the clothes dryer. My siblings and I would watch Momma wash clothes in a wash tub using a wash board. (Now, if you haven't seen one, there is a set of such tools at the Smith Robertson Museum in Jackson, MS or at the Caring n' Sharing School in Madison, MS.)

As I was saying, we stood by while Momma washed a large pile of dirty clothes in a metal wash tub, thirty-six-inches-in diameter. She rubbed a bar of Octagon soap on one piece of clothing at a time on the wash board. Using an up and down motion on the wash board that was designed with about twenty horizonal crinkled rows of metal enclosed in a wood encasement, that was how we washed clothes. When the clothes appeared clean, Momma passed them to me to rinse in a black iron pot of water, depending on the color of the clothes. If the clothes were white, they got a blue-rinse that was created with a blue tablet that diffused in the water prior to rinsing. I was in charge of that pot. If the clothes were colored, they got a cool rinse in clear water. A younger sibling was in charge of that pot. From that process, my siblings and I rang out the pieces and placed them on the barbed-wire clothes line—no clothes pins until years later. Barbed wire was made of metal with metal sharp spurs spaced about a foot apart. Farmers used barbed wire to fence in their pastures to deter livestock from breaking out. However, we used it to hold the clothes on the line without clothes pins. If we weren't careful hanging out the clothes, the spurs could cut a one-fourth inch slit on a finger or hand. Okay, you understand the chore, right?

At the time, I didn't know the health advantages of hanging out clothes. So, now I know we were blessed even before we knew it. We learned later in life that hanging out laundry gets one outside and the sunlight can alleviate depression, improve immunity, increase social relationships, and more? That could explain why we were so happy. We later learned that line-dried clothes also help prolong the life of the clothing. (Experts say the rolling and tumbling of damp laundry take its toll on the fibers in clothing and bedding.) Also, sunlight is a good bleach and a disinfectant. Line-drying helps remove stains without adding chemical agents to the wash. The downside is sunlight can also cause fading; therefore, we learned to hang color clothes in a shady area.

And lastly, we learned that the scent of line-dried laundry is better than the expensive laundry detergents that try to imitate the smell. That's why we country children smelled good even though we took one full "washtub" bath on weekends and face-towel touchups between times. We, of course, sealed our freshness with Baking Soda for deodorant.

We had fun with the clothesline too. Sometimes the younger siblings played hide and seek with the clothes on the line. When they hid the top half of the body behind the clothes, they thought the whole body was hidden. (The bottom half of the body was visible.) They didn't understand how I could find them so quickly, and they had difficulty finding me.

The lesson embedded here is being poor without modern conveniences can have benefits.

A Serious Side of the Country Lifestyle

Our family was taught early to be truthful with each other

in play and in business. I'm not talking about the innocence of childhood games, but of childhood relationships. If, for example, a sibling borrowed a dime to purchase candy. (*Borrow* means you plan to return to the lender whatever was received.) If the process is not complete and the lender does not get the dime promised, our parents used this as an opportunity to teach honesty and responsibility. Some adults figure that children don't have to be taught responsibility, but that virtue begins in childhood.

Other lessons some parents should not teach, however, is the practice of sinning. For example, a few of our country neighbors committed sins in secret, or out of sight. Years later, neighbors and even school children, noticed some of their playmates looked more like a man across the neighborhood than the man they claimed was their "father." In conversation, some of the same people try to convince themselves and others in saying, "We don't understand why children are so wild these days. We take them to church, and they act like they never saw the inside of a church."

There are some exceptions, but generally those children who grow up with moral and truthful precepts and examples before them, will NOT stray very far from the lifestyle of the parents, especially if BOTH parents are demonstrating the same lifestyle. In other words, "The chip doesn't fall far from the tree." (Modified by family from Proverbs 22:6 (KJV of the Holy Bible).

I think the ugliness of hypocrisy was personified by what I witnessed in my community. I was so disturbed by what I saw folks doing; folks I thought were Christians. I had to decide whether to get bitter or better because of the hypocrisy I saw in the church. I chose to be better and pledged to be real, so help me God.

I don't know the *whys* or the *how-comes* but, after much thought, I'm inclined to believe that God orchestrated my life, circumstances and experiences to prepare me for such a time as this. I don't remember being persuaded or trying to have a *mind to do right and go straight*. To me, it has always been a demonstrated lifestyle of my parents that appeared to be more attractive than those influences outside of my home.

I was about nine when Bishop Charles Price Jones died in 1949. I wanted to be *good and right* with God like my grandparents portrayed Bishop Jones to be. I wanted to know more. I heard the sadness in my Big Momma's voice when she heard of his passing. I sensed a great loss and a spirit of "What are we going to do without the leading of that Man of God who loved righteousness and hated SIN!"

When I was almost twelve, Momma said with motherly conviction: "It's time for you to make a decision to be a Christian. When you do, there will be a change, and you will know there is a change."

Just as Moses had the "burning bush" experience on the far side of the wilderness (Exodus 3:1-17, KJV), I felt "I had to be alone on the far side of the cow pasture in a designated place;" the way Momma described. I found a nice plum bush and placed a five-gallon can under it and sat while I read my Bible. I prayed and read from Psalms. When I exalted my energy from sitting, I looked around to see if I saw a change in the sky or something spectacular. I thought I'd see chariots flying over on the clouds. Momma said there would be a change! A personal encounter (I Cor. 5:17).

I placed a rock under the bush with my name on it so that I would begin again the next day at the same spot until my change came. This ritual occurred for three days. "This rock will be here for my children and generations to come and they will know this is where the change came; that I made a spiritual transition here." I pondered in my heart.

I thought it was my time to decide; make a line of demarcation from the old to the new life in Christ. In our family, each child was expected to make this "rites of passage" around age twelve, like Jesus who went to the temple at that age. Momma always excused her children from all chores during this time so they could be alone with God without distractions.

Nevertheless, I felt pressured because I didn't see a flying chariot or anything to help me decide. Unlike boys and girls in the

Baptist church, during revival, the candidates sat on the Mourners' Bench—boys on one side and girls on the other. Preachers pranced in front of them, shouting the old testament stories and begging them to accept Christ. The Baptist candidates attended two services a day for two weeks to digest Bible lessons and have plenty time to decide. The congregation would spice up the spirit by singing the Charlie Watts hymns where one leads with a verse and the congregation followed, repeating the same words. This was community revival!

In the Holiness church, the candidates sat together on the first pews. Because the Baptist church was closer than our church, sometimes Momma would take us to hear the Baptist sermons. Also, she still enjoyed those Baptist hymns she grew up with before marrying my daddy and joining the Holiness church. However, she would tell us that we will visit the Baptist churches, but join the family church at New Lake Church of Christ Holiness even if we made the Big Decision at the Baptist Church.

I realized I would be making an individual decision to accept what Jesus did for me on the Cross, and committing to serve God the rest of my life. I remember thinking that if I ever become a Christian, I will NOT be a hypocrite.

My change came in July 1952.   My change moved me from just "self" to include my neighbors. I went to pray every day on my five-gallon can; three times a day, like Daniel.

After our respective decisions, my siblings and I would be taken to the family's church, New Lake Church in Jackson, MS to make a public confession and get baptized. We didn't get baptized in a pond like some of our neighbors, but in a concrete outdoor pool with steps that went down into the water. (We felt modern, not better— just not muddy.) The church members sang the hymn, "Take me to the water, take me to the water, take to the water to be baptized."

When we returned home, our mother Lucile, would talk with us about her special acceptance of Christ at age nine. She described how she flew up from the Mourners' Bench into the preacher's arms, saying, "I'm ready to live for Jesus!" She felt a new kind of joy that was uncontrollable and indescribable. She shared the good news with her mother who was not present in the service at the time. Her mother's disappointing response was, "Huh hum." She did not share her new found life in Christ.

Lucile's mother, Mary, was not comfortable with anyone being happy. The one-half Choctaw-Indian mother would whip my Momma Lucile and her eight siblings even when they had done nothing wrong. Her mother's philosophy was constant: "I'm whipping you so you will always be good." Momma, Lucile, didn't know what to do because being good wasn't working. Also, being saved was not a FREE ticket from whippings. Momma received another undeserved whipping the following day. Momma prayed and taught me to pray.

When I got saved, I found the truth, I enjoyed saying the right things, doing the right things, seeing and touching the right things suitable for my age. My parents rejoiced with me. If I sensed something that was not right, something inside of me bubbled up like a warning sign, STOP! Don't go there! Or, proceed with caution. I liked the new creature that I became, and I still enjoy the Christian journey. The Christianity life is not an event, but a journey of events.

I entered Burgess High in the ninth grade around this time. I told a few friends about my new life with Christ, but not the whole class. Some didn't think it was a cool thing to do.

*First Row, l. to r.: Dean Carey, Annie M. Webster, Mary H. Cole, Dorothy Green, **Jannie Ballard**, Lillie R. McClenty, Edna M. Gooden. Second Row: L. R. McMullan, teacher; Nepolean M. McClenty, Eva M. Griffin, Willie B. Thompson, Lula P. Luckett, B. C. Johnson, Solomon Green, George Vaughn, Willie C. Hodge, Mamie Franklin. Third Row: Jimmie L. Smith, Hattie Cameron, Katie B. Luckett, Annette Haggard, Arthur Burns, Willie L. Walker, Oree Jones, Paul Brooks, Ernest Hinton, and Mary Brown.*

My principal, Mr. Walter R. Burgess, always knew how to validate each student. He encouraged, expected much, and held us accountable. He was a tall, handsome man, who demonstrated professionalism in every way, every day. He was a visible and vocal example of an educator. He and his wife, Myrtle K. lived on the Burgess High school campus that was named after him. Their two children, Nancy and Walter, Jr., represented them well with good behavior and good grades. *I remember what I saw, and what I heard.*

- 7 -

Our Home and Family of Ten

What is worse than having no food, clothes or
shelter? It's when you have NO dreams,
NO ambition, NO hope for the future? – Bit
of Wisdom, Caring n' Sharing School

Our house was a typical country cottage. We lived way off the public road. The man-made road was created from regular use by walking farmers and trails made by wagons.

The county didn't cut roads for African-American people during the early 1900s. Therefore, when you wanted to come to our house, you would come about 500 feet off the public road to Mrs. Wiggins's house. Pass her house and follow a wagon trail through the woods for about a mile, come through a pasture fence to a little white house with a porch. You entered the house from the porch's doorway with windows on either side to a short hallway. The backside of the hallway was a curtain-covered cut-off with shelves that formed a large clothes closet for the whole family. There was one bedroom to the left and one on the right.

Each bedroom had a fireplace. The children stayed in the room on the right which also opened to a small dining room and kitchen. There was also a small back porch leading out from the kitchen. In the center of the kitchen was the wood-burning oven. To the right was a tall cupboard that looked like the one in most Nursery Rhyme books with "Old Mother Hubbard" who went to her cupboard. A wood box filled with wood chips and pieces set conveniently beside the cupboard under the back window that was draped with white-gathered curtains. A small table was in front of the cupboard next to the door that connected to the dining area.

Our *food* was grown on the truck farm, and we sold extra vegetables to acquire funds to purchase what we could not grow such as flour, seasonings, and some meats. Some meats such as chickens and pork were also grown on the farm. Grandma Janie had a smoke house where she smoked the pork hams, bacon and sausage. During the winter months, we made sandwiches for school because our schoolhouse didn't have a kitchen or lunchroom. Salt meats were fried for breakfast and lunch when available.

Water for us came primarily from a cistern. Most country people today don't use that method of acquiring water due to the level of pollution. However, in our day, fathers would work together to dig a deep hole about six feet in diameter; then, pour concrete in the bottom and upward to seal the walls. Now, when the rain came off the roof of the house through the gutter it was inserted to empty into the tin-covered cistern. A larger hole was cut into the tin cover of the cistern so that a bucket could be lowered on a rope to draw water out for use.

Sometimes during a draught, we used water from our water well which was about one-fourth of a mile from the house. It was located where the Well Finder located the water level. A Well Finder is one who could come to one's property with a small "Y" shaped tree branch. The Well Finder would skillfully hold the branch firmly and the branch would supernaturally lead the Finder to the spot where water would be found. At that location is where the well would be dug. The men took turns digging with a pick and shovel until a hole was ten to fifteen feet deep and about three feet wide. They chipped away the dirt and threw it out as long as it was a shallow hole. Then, when it was too deep to throw out, a foot tub would be lowered for the dirt to be loaded into it and drawn up by the helpers on top. This process continued until they hit a water vein that would be seeping in on the feet of the digger. Then, it was time to draw water out of the well and allow water to flow.

Now, about our clothes supply: we purchased second-hand clothes with the money we made from helping neighbors chop and pick their cotton. Momma purchased clothes from "off the street" in Jackson where people had racks of used clothes for sale. Seldom did they have used shoes that would fit our feet. Therefore, our parents had to purchase new shoes with acquired money from the sale of herbs, vegetables and other money saved from picking cotton for neighborhood farmers.

Even though that money was limited, it didn't deter Dad from his set of priorities. My father stopped raising cotton when Monroe, his second son, was born. He foretold that cotton would drain our family of valuable time when we should be in school.

Case in point: Sometimes the only children in school would be the Ballard children and sometimes the teachers' children. Looking back, the most successful children coming out of our community were those families who sacrificed the cotton fields and allowed their children to go to school when it started in September. Many children did not start school until after the cotton was picked, sometimes at the end of October.

However, some exceptional children never learned to read well. In our community, there were sons of very skilled carpenters who were academically challenged. However, they learned carpentry work. Their eyes were trained to "eyeball" measurements as accurately as a person with pencil and paper. They made a living building houses including one with ten rooms.

My parents valued education and work, but, for us, they kept them in that order. As youngsters, they taught us to value education more than work. They believed that it was all right to work hard to be educated. But don't sacrifice education for work unless you are the main source of survival for your family.

My father didn't want to take a chance on our making a living without an education. As mentioned earlier, my first school, built by my grandfather and community leaders, had limited resources. My father also served as the principal (without pay), rented extra farm land to neighbors at about the cost of taxes, served as the community doctor, and shared his farming expertise as needed.

If a child had difficulty learning to read (like my brother Monroe), he just wore extra coats so that the whippings wouldn't be so painful. Most of our teachers were high school graduates, but had better-educated supervisors who monitored the instruction. We all learned to sight read (a.k.a rote read), but somehow, we mastered the skill well enough to acquire college degrees and above.

My parents desired that all eight children would at least finish college before marrying. Momma's stand was that we all must get married before sex or having children. Both were good principled goals, but the children had to take ownership for them to materialize.

Therefore, our parents taught us a principle to guide us: "Do right, go straight; that's what it takes." Dad and Momma firmly believed if they taught us biblical principles of morality and practiced prayerfully making their decisions, we, the children, would do *about* the same.

Dad said *about the same* because most youth learn from seeing first their parents as role models; then later, they make decisions on their own. My parents trusted that we would build on what we learned at home before venturing out.

Our dad always said he wanted to have enough children so they would have playmates and not have to find friends in the community. He didn't feel the lifestyle of some families in the community would be a positive influence on his young children. When we didn't get a ride to New Lake Church of Christ Holiness in Jackson, MS, we held church at home. At the close of the family church service, Momma and Dad prayed for each of us. Then, their prayers were followed by each one of the children's little prayers. It was something we still remember with special reverence.

My relationship with my dad began to improve with age and with a desire to obey parents without murmuring.

I noticed that Dad went out early in the morning, so one day I followed him to see what he was doing. He had the Bible with him. When he came to a big oak tree, he sat on the ground and opened the Bible. He read for a long time, it seemed. Then he knelt and placed pieces of paper in a circle around him and prayed, touching each piece. He sometimes took other books with him like the *Books of Moses*. He talked with God, not pleading and shouting, but making petitions before the "throne;" declaring, but not emotional.

I thought it was strange. So, one day I asked him, "Dad, why do you pray like that? You know, using all the books, papers and stuff?"

He said nothing at first; then said, "I talk to God about each one of you. All your names are on the papers that encircle me." He rested his hand on my shoulder, and walked silently to the house.

The next day, I felt blessed as I went to the New Spring Hill School about one mile away that was recently built by the County. We no longer went to the Ballard Chapel that was also Spring Hill Elementary during the week.

Now, I admired my dad even more after my "Plum Bush" salvation experience and after I learned that my name was on one of those pieces of paper on which he prayed every day.

Dad was a nurturing father. It was easier for me to talk to him. Momma was okay, but quick to respond and may not have heard the whole story before she gave advice. Dad was a better listener. Sometimes I only knew he heard me when he responded with a sudden quiet grunt, "Hun huh."

Momma was different. For example, one day I asked Momma where babies came from. She went a long way around to associate it with my menstrual periods. I still don't remember exactly how she explained it. I had terrible headaches associated with the monthly periods. So, "Does that have something to do with babies?" I pondered. I told Dad about it, and he told me to go back to Momma and she'd explain what was happening in my body. She summed it up this way: "You are a woman now. Your monthly bleedings mean your body is ready to develop and produce a baby. So, keep boys' hands off you because you can get pregnant. Socialize with boys with a "long handle spoon."

Wow! That was my sex education. If boys touch you, you could have a baby.

Principally speaking, Momma was a Christian and a good mother. But sometimes she was unable to keep promises made in business. Like the times when we picked cotton for Mr. Coker.

She told me I could have all the money made above 200 pounds of cotton. Getting three dollars per hundred, I would get three dollars if I picked 200! I was excited. I wanted to learn how to pick more than two hundred pounds.

A neighbor, Mattie Collins, heard of my interest and decided to teach me the secret. She said, "Most people try to pick two rows of cotton at a time but turning from one row to another will waste time. The best way is to pick one row at a time and start at the bottom of the stalk and come to the top."

I used that strategy and began to pick two hundred regularly. Momma changed what she said about giving me the amount over 200 pounds. She explained that she wanted to reward me that way, but money was tight. She needed the extra money to help buy everybody clothes for school. I was disappointed but understood my Momma's concerns. I decided to continue working hard to help out.

I continued to pick as much as I could, getting up to 300 pounds on some days. Momma appreciated my help, but gave me only a fraction of what she had promised. She was not thinking of the effect that change had on me, but it was demotivating. I was working harder, picking at least 225 pounds before earning any extra money. I cried silently, and did not know how to explain my feelings to my mother. She was trying hard to make extra money to provide basic needs for eight children and supplement income from Dad's herbal sales that were sometimes slow and unstable, especially in the winter months.

This was not the only time I pitched in to help family. We were always short on cash. No one had a public job and we were not making much money from peddling vegetables and herbs in the city. One idea was that my second oldest brother Monroe, now seventeen, was old enough to get a public job. He would ride with Uncle Nathan Wiggins who had a job and a car. That green 1949 Plymouth was the possession of a well-to-do uncle, we thought. He agreed to let Monroe ride with him.

Back at home, we had a problem. Monroe did all the plowing on the truck farm. Now, with a day job he would not be able to plow. Without hesitation, I said, "I'll do it." I had committed to plowing while Monroe worked in town. That was a big task for a fifteen-year-old girl, but I learned quickly. The main lessons were to practice the "horse language" used in plowing such as *haw* and *get-up*! The mule learned my voice quickly also, and obeyed while plowing in a straight line.

I remember walking behind the mules. Can't say how much I got done but I was working. The rows weren't always straight, but they all went in the same direction.

Soon Monroe lost his job for being under age, they said. He got another job but later lost it for asking for a raise. That night, I could tell something was wrong when he came home. He squinted his eyes like the lights were too bright. He was squinting and keeping his head down. He didn't know how to tell Momma but somehow, we, his siblings, found out and teased Monroe for losing two jobs in a row. He asked Momma to tell us to leave him alone. We did, but he had to tell Momma the whole sorry story of how it happened.

Monroe was always trusted to do more than most teens his age. I remember the time my dad borrowed a neighbor's truck to take us to New Lake Church in Jackson for a Children's Day program. Monroe had only a few lessons driving anything besides a wagon, but Dad trusted him to drive the truck loaded with his siblings—most sitting on the bed of the truck. The smallest ones rode with Momma and Dad in the cab. When coming to a deep curve, Monroe lost control of the truck and it went into a ditch. He put the truck in reverse and succeeded in getting it back out but the front fender was bent. Dad used a crowbar from under the cab seat to pull the fender off the wheel so we could drive to our destination, New Lake Church.

At first, we thought we were going to return home, but Dad said, "No, you all have been memorizing your speeches to be on program, and that is exactly what will happen." We went to New Lake Church, jumped down off the truck, dusted off our clothes and wiped our faces with a damp "rag" Momma brought for that purpose. We said our speeches "nice and loud" like Momma taught us.

The next day, Dad returned the truck to Mr. Webster, our neighbor, and told him that we would pay for the damages to his truck. It was costly, but Dad kept his word.

———————◆———————

BIT OF WISDOM:

If you control your life, you can plan your future. If you manage what you have today, you can have for tomorrow, too. National speaker, Les Brown says it this way: "Do what is easy today, your life will be hard; but do what is hard today, your future life will be easy."

- 8 -

The Family Home Burns

To do right and go straight, it takes a stout heart. –Jannie Johnson

Life was good for the Ballards; sort of good until our home burned. We were poor, but just didn't know we were poor. We had little money but lots of attention from our parents. We were happy because we had each other.

My dad, Seth, set some priorities for his family that were wise, but different for the time in which we lived. The Ballards were the only family in the neighborhood that didn't raise cotton. We were the only children attending school most days, especially during the first week of school. Our peers worked the fields.

This year things were a little different. The county offered summer school at Spring Hill Consolidated School, responding to an unspoken request to provide summer school for the children in the county who worked the fields and missed a few months of school. Even though this was not the case with my siblings and me, Dad decided, anyway, to send us to summer school.

This came as no surprise to us who had often heard our dad make a point to Momma that education was a priority in our home. He was often heard saying, "My children are going to get an education. Cotton is here now, but it will be gone. We can't depend on making a living with cotton."

Even though the Ballards were not cotton farmers, my dad allowed us to make extra money by helping other farmers when school was not in session. His notion seemed strange to Momma because she couldn't imagine cotton NOT being the king of the South. But the children knew that education was valued in the home.

Getting the clothes ready for school was a year-long endeavor for the Ballard children. Weekly trips to town were two-fold: (1) sell vegetables and herbs; and (2) make purchases of food and find bargain clothing for the family.

Everyone got up early, getting ready for summer school. "You know we have to leave by 7 AM to make that one-mile walk to school. We want to be on time at this new Spring Hill school." Monroe firmly reminded everyone.

Monroe, a tall and precocious pre-teen about twelve, was the man in charge of rounding everyone up for school. This task came natural for him. He made his rounds through the whitewashed, five-room house yelling, "Let's go, let's go now, or you will be left. No time to waste!"

But this morning was special somehow. The brilliant streams of sunlight through the ceiling-to-floor windows embraced with white, laced curtains gave witness to the expected temperature for the day—hot and humid. The freshly scrubbed wood floors and fluffed corn shuck mattress beds draped with white, Clorox-bleached sheets claimed attention in an unusual way. Somehow, it made me feel blessed.

We left for our one-mile walk to school, arriving on time as Monroe predicted and planned. With fewer children enrolled in summer school, it was commonplace for us to have one-on-one instruction. Assignments were completed at school; no homework. It was also a chance to play on the big school yard without bullies. We felt special to be allowed to walk next door to the country store, buy snacks and enjoy the rare occasion of chewing and blowing bubble gum.

During recess, an unusual scene caught the children's attention. An extremely dark stream of smoke was whooshing into the sky at a distance in the southeastern direction, the direction of the

Ballards' home. Someone observed, "Looks like someone's house is burning." Yet, we continued to play.

After we were settled back in class, a neighbor beckoned for the teacher and quietly conferred with her outside the classroom door. The children listened to hear who might be in trouble for something. Instead, they overheard the neighbor say: "I came to let the Ballard children know that their house has burned down. All was lost, but no one was burned or hurt. Please excuse them. I'll walk them home."

The Ballard children were corralled quickly. The older children in summer school were notified of the fire first. We ran and walked, ran and walked. Our long-legged brother, Monroe, led the pack home. We scampered under barbed wire fences, crossed pastures, taking the shortest route to our house. We hurried along in disbelief, crying, screaming silently, feeling alone in the world because we Ballards didn't feel very popular in the community.

"Who will help us? We have no friends!" were the thoughts that raced through our minds. We didn't want to believe the bad news, but the rising black smoke was telling.

Simultaneously, Willie Jordan and James "Main" Collins went through the neighborhood running and screaming, "Seth's house is on fire! See that black smoke going up over the trees! It's his house! We must go help!" People dropped what they were doing and joined the caring mob of neighbors.

Aunt Mamie Wiggins was two-months pregnant when she saw them running. She grabbed her two older sons, Thomas (*Blessed Bones*) and Pete, and ran tugging them along. She dropped them off at Mrs. Wiggins's house as she ran almost breathless to help save her sister's burning house. When she arrived, the house was completely engulfed. No fire department was even close, only neighbors.

Someone asked Momma, "Don't you have a young son? Where is your baby son?"

Momma's eyes stretched in startled panic. "Oh, mercy! I hope he's not in there!" She nervously and swiftly ran toward the burning house calling, "Sook? Sook?" She cried the louder. "Sook!" (Sook is the nickname for my baby brother Sylvester.)

Someone held her back from the fire. Suddenly, there was a faint response from behind the nearby bushes, "Ma'am." Sook was hiding because of his misjudgment that no one knew about except him. He had accidentally started the fire.

"Ma'am," answered again the frightened little Sylvester ("Sook"). Everyone gave a sigh of relief. Momma went to hug him and asked him, "What happened, Sook?" She knew that she had sent him to rekindle the wood fire but that may not have been a wise assignment for a three-year-old. Sook told her with teary eyes how he tried to stop the fire but couldn't. He was thinking he would be punished so he ran out and hid. She didn't punish him.

"What caused the fire?" Someone asked.

"It's really my fault," replied Momma. "I was on the porch sewing together pieces to make quilts for the winter. I knew the fire was probably getting low in the stove where I had a pot of beans cooking for supper. So, I sent Sook to rekindle the fire in the woodburning stove. He put a hand full of paper from the wood box to help re-start the fire. Sook said a half-lit piece of paper fell out of the fire chamber (oven door). He quickly picked up the fallen paper and rushed it over to the wood box. Before the paper burned out, it latched on to the curtain that hang lowly over the wood box. Frightened, little three-year-old "Sook" ran outside to hide. In minutes, maybe seconds, Momma said she smelled smoke and rushed to find the kitchen totally engulfed in flames. She was frantic and devastated. She awakened Dad who was taking an afternoon nap that usually followed his morning garden work of plowing and chopping the crop. "He tried to grab a few vital items, but ran out without shoes." Momma recalled.

There was no large water source to draw from to quench the fire and no fire department to call. They could only watch the house go up in flames.

Screams, and murmurings of sadness penetrated the air from family and neighbors who saw the serious smoke. Heat, smoke, crackling sounds, sweat and misery describe the long hours of that July day in 1952. Our dad stood taller than most around—trying to be *strong*. Some neighbors had come to help, others came to steal what was left from the fire. Several people found coins in the ashes and felt they had found a gold mine.

We heard that the Red Cross would help us resettle somewhere since we had nothing saved except a chest-of-drawer. However, we only received some oversized adult clothes that almost fit no one.

There was a gentle tap on Dad's shoulder. He turned and looked into the face of Aunt Mamie, his sister-in-law.

"Have you decided on a place to stay, yet?" She asked sympathetically.

"No," Dad responded mechanically without feeling. "I don't know anywhere my family and I can stay."

His strong commanding voice was quiet, almost a whisper. He had felt almost independent up to this point in his life. He only looked to God to deliver. Now he, Seth Ballard, Sr., a man of God was homeless, and felt helpless. Now, he was at the mercy and free offerings of others.

My Aunt Mamie continues, "I will check with my mother-in-law, Mattie Wiggins, to see if you all can use the vacant house next door to hers."

"Would you?" responded Dad and Momma in concert.

I'll walk by there on my way home and let you know what she says later this evening. She did just that.

Mrs. Wiggins allowed us to stay there until something better came along. In the meantime, Dad was checking out the vacated two-room schoolhouse that his father built in 1917. He would see if that building could serve as our temporary home until we enlarged and renovated it to accommodate our nine-member family. Nine, because Seth, the oldest, was just accepted at Piney Woods, a boarding school.

The children's scholarships to Piney Woods were blessings prayed for. We didn't realize this house-burning tragedy was a blessing in disguise that Momma had prayed for when she asked God to give her a home beside a public road—out of the backwoods.

(But, let's not discuss that now. Let's follow what happened next.)

"I reckon that living in Mrs. Wiggins's old vacant house will do for now," Dad said reluctantly. I know I can't house my family in either of the cribs—one's filled with remnants of last fall's corn and the other with odd items. The old retail store/smoke house near the house was severely damaged by the fire," he continued.

The flames became shorter and shorter while the smoke followed suit.

My father, Herb Doctor Seth Ballard, in total disbelief, moved closer to what was his home for all his life and the birthplace of his eight children. He led the curious bystanders to different viewing positions. They walked slowly and cautiously to see if there was anything salvageable.

The remaining neighbors made customary offerings like. "Let me know if I can help." "We have some extra stuff to get you started again." "Is there anyone you'd like us to talk to about what happened?"

Dad's responses to the half-heard questions and comments were brief signs of gratitude and barely audible: "All right. Yes ... Okay ... Um huh. Thank you."

The happenings of the moments, minutes, hours were so unreal. This was too hard to absorb. He just stood staring. The reflections of the tragedy were flickering in the pupils of his strong penetrating eyes. Time kept ticking but for him life stood still. Jarred into reality by the soft hand of his three- year-old son patting him on his thigh, he looked down at the face of innocence gazing up at his dad for forgiveness and comfort. He wanted to let Dad know he was sorry for the role he played in starting the fire, but the words wouldn't come out.

Instead, he asked, "Dad, you okay?"

"Um huh." Then rested his hand briefly on Sook's little shoulder. They walked together around the smoldering ashes. They took slow steps as if testing the stability of the earth beneath their feet. Little Sook felt a little less scared now. They continued their walk. The two chimneys came in full view, the cribs, the partially damaged retail store, the trees, gardens, yard, remnants of iron post beds, metal pieces from mattress springs, the iron stove, things after eight hours, still smoking. Seth paused almost in the spot he stood the day before but with a more reverent demeanor. Yesterday's nightmare was mingled with rays of hope. He took a deep breath and gave a sign of relief. He thought, "The circumstances are the same, but I have had an inward change." He took the baby boy, Sook, back to the temporary red imitation brick house where others were getting settled.

Seth returned before dark to make sure the fire did not spread during the night. Then there was something else. He continued the walk he had earlier. This time it was with God Himself. He was led to walk around the burned home seven times. Like Joshua in the Bible. He looked across the once flowered front yard that had become trampled and blanked with parts of burnt tin roofing. He viewed the fruit and nuts orchard that was planted by his grandmother, Laura Ballard. She had what they called a "green thumb." Everything she planted seem to grow and produce. We enjoyed her pear trees, apple trees, peach trees, and pecan trees producing various sizes of pecans. He reflected on his childhood experiences through the present. Then said, "Lord, I thank you for all you have done for me and my family through the years ... You brought us through all that; I trust you to bring us through this."

Our dad was divinely guided to make a home of the schoolhouse that his father and neighbors built for the community at the turn of the twentieth century. God seemed to smile on the land. Cultivating and vegetation made the land fertile. Crops yielded beyond imagination and expectations that year. The schoolhouse would be transformed into our new home with two fireplaces, a big kitchen, a long porch and two bedrooms.

Everyone adjusted, and the children had more friends than ever at school. Even Momma and Dad were encouraged by the support of our neighbors.

My dad, Seth, meditated underneath the shade of a walnut tree in the back yard on the bed of a wagon. Somehow, he felt inner peace.

This Photo by Unknown Author is licensed under CC BY-SA
Under a similar walnut tree, near our homeplace,
my dad prayed and meditated.

- 9 -

Old Spring Hill School Becomes Our Home

You cannot keep me in the dark unless you can put out all the lights.
From Bits of Wisdom, Caring n' Sharing School

With thumbs hanging in his two front work pant pockets, he looked to the east where he had expected God to do miracles for two generations. Then, my dad slowly looked toward the sky inspecting the position of the sun, now tilting toward the west. He estimated five more hours of daylight.

He said, "Let's go y'all." With more body language than verbal, the family followed my dad's lead in moving in the direction of the temporary housing. We walked almost single file down the path through the woods to the little red-imitation-brick-siding house that was brushed out and cleaned by helpful neighbors.

Walking to the last fence beside the pasture where the cows were grazing, the family meandered through the woods on pass Mrs. Wiggins' gardens until they came to her doorsteps. She greeted us briefly with directions on how to best use the house she and neighbors had prepared for us. This empty dwelling was a welcomed sight for the tired, hot feet and weary bodies. Neighbors and friends also pitched in to assure we had some food, water, coal oil lamps and pallets to sleep on.

The trees cast their shadows onto the front porch of this little red house followed by night sounds—crickets and frogs squawking in rhythmic relays. Turning in was simple for the Ballard family this evening—no distractions; we had nothing.

The children fell asleep with more questions than there were answers, but not Dad.

At 2 AM, Dad was still wide awake. He pulled up from his pallet and walked through the front door onto the squeaky front porch. He stepped off the porch and admired the brilliant almost daylight radiance of the full moon. Its splendor, just for a moment, took him away from his time of distress. He knelt and prayed. He petitioned and questioned God.

"I have walked upright with you, Lord. I have given my whole life to you. I have done what I thought you wanted me to do. Why? Why am I kneeling before you homeless? Why am I tonight not knowing what to do? Why do I feel forsaken?" He questioned God.

Something some religious people say one should not do.

Just when he felt there would be no answer, a feeling of heartfelt peace came over him. He rose to his feet and faced the East. A warm sensation enclosed his body. He stood still and the cacophony of the moment yielded to silence. A serene presence enfolded him. He was motionless. God spoke, and he listened.

"You are blessed among men. You have asked and I have rewarded you according to your faith. I gave you the wife you asked for, and you didn't ask me why or how? I gave you eight healthy, intelligent children. You didn't ask me why? I directed the time and place for you to meet Dr. Laurence C. Jones, President of Piney Woods School, who gave each of your children scholarships to his school that will take them from elementary to junior college without charge—not even the charge for uniforms that they must wear. You didn't ask me why, right? So, where is your faith now, my son?"

"I blessed your crops year after year and provided food for your table. I clothed you and your family, and all these blessings did not move you to question my favor to you over others.

"When I gave you the opportunity to finish high school at Christ Missionary and Industrial College of the Church of Christ

Holiness (USA), and later to enter Alcorn Agricultural College to learn a trade, you trusted me." The quiet voice continued.

"All the years of your life, I have guided you. I have kept you well, strong and in good health as you learned about herbs for medicinal purposes from a 103-year-old ex-slave who I directed to you. You learned how to serve your people when they were not served by the white doctors at that time. You were there to help them and I was there to help you; to give you wisdom to know what to do. Now, son, trust my love for you and trust what I am about to do. This difficult experience will change your whole family's life." God said in a whisper.

Dad broke the silence and spoke out loud.

"My God, I yield. I humble myself before you. I will continue to seek your face your presence and directions. Thank you, Lord. And my dad peacefully dropped off to sleep.

The next day, a load of sharecroppers from Mr. Gus Greens plantation came with lumber, hammers and nails, picks and shovels to help transform the old Spring Hill schoolhouse into a home. Mr. Green was one of the rich African-American men in the community. He also pulled in his friend Mr. Willie Adams, a neighbor who had carpentry skills. Mr. Adams also rented acreage from our dad for his cotton crop.

"Seth, we are here to work on your house. We heard you wanted to remodel the old schoolhouse and dig a cistern for water?

"Right." Dad replied. "But I don't have a way to buy supplies and things."

"We have that covered," said Mr. Gus Green, the rich African-American landlord with trucks and many resources.

So, the next day they picked up Dad in the loaded truck of supplies and headed for the old schoolhouse to remodel. A group of strong men dug a big hole and walled it up with concrete to form the cistern while the others transformed the old schoolhouse.

We, the children, missed school two days because we didn't have changing clothes and other needed stuff. We sat around and studied our schoolbooks that we cherished. Momma would supervise and help us when she could. But most times, she was sorting out things that neighbors had brought us.

Dad and the men were working hard on the schoolhouse—boarding up some of the windows that were previously designed for light during school hours and church on Sundays. They divided one of the large rooms into two bedrooms—one for Momma and Dad and the other for the six children—three per bed. Three girls for one bed and three boys were in the other. Rosa, the oldest girl, had recently joined Seth, the oldest, at Piney Woods.

One classroom became the kitchen and dining area, but space was still limited. A fireplace was placed in our parents' room on the end, but the middle room had no source of heat.

Winters were bitter and cold. Dad and the older siblings would go to the woods to cut firewood for the kitchen oven and the fireplaces.

Dad started making plans for enlarging the square footage. By the summer he had gathered enough lumber to add on three more rooms on the southside of the original school building. We now had space for the girls to have a room and the boys to have a room.

Everyone was excited about the proposed plans to have more space. That excitement was interrupted when we heard about a scheduled visit from our mostly northern aunts and uncles who wanted to divide the Ballard property and sell their individual portions.

Progress Can Hurt Loved Ones

I was about twelve or thirteen when my aunts and uncles decided that it was time to divide up their inherited land from their parents, Nelson and Janie Ballard around 1953. My dad, Seth Ballard, was the only one living in MS. He was the one who kept up the home place, paid the taxes and assisted with their mother, Janie Ballard until she moved to St. Louis to live with her daughter, Janie Ballard Lowe who was in a better position to care for Grandma Janie in her waning years.

During the decision-making to divide the land and sell or not,

I was impressed with my dad's sense of responsibility and loyalty to the inheritance. To me, he was a great man, but, my aunts and uncles raised their voices in contempt. They talked as if he were the dummy of the family because he stayed in MS, particularly in rural Madison County with a plenty of nothingness.

My dad was trying to persuade them to sell the land to him over time, and he would pay the taxes as well. "No, no," they shouted, "We want to get rid of the land because we are not coming back to Mississippi."

"But what if your children want to live in Mississippi after they grow up? They would own property and could build a house." He pleaded.

"No! Seth, we are going to sell, and we have a buyer, Mr. James "Main" Collins is willing to buy the land on Coker Road at thirty-five dollars an acre." Also, Rev. Charlie Jordan wants to buy the portion on Robinson Springs Rd, Pocahontas, MS. (now Madison, MS). The family agreed to sell the land, but none of the mineral rights.

All agreed to sell to Mr. Collins and Rev. Jordan except Uncle Sylvester. He said he would sell his portion to our Dad. Our family ended up with forty plus acres of land.

Plans to Build Extra Rooms

After the land settlement, we resumed our plans to build extra rooms on our house. Neighbors pitched in giving a few hours of free labor while Dad and Monroe worked diligently.

Now, it's the late 1950s. Electricity was coming to the rural areas. We wanted the new rooms to have electricity along with the original rooms. Monroe went to work with an electrician for a few days as an apprentice so he could learn how to help wire the house. When the three additional rooms were added, Monroe was ready to complete the whole job. He learned quickly and the electrician went with him to Jackson to buy the supplies needed. Monroe, at age sixteen, wired the three additional rooms!

We were so excited that we could start saving to buy a real

electric refrigerator. We could do away with the ice box for which we had to wave down a traveling iceman to purchase a chunk of ice. We could only keep perishable as long as the ice lasted. We could also do away with the coal oil lamps and portable Aladdin lamps around which we studied and completed our homework.

The problem was, we were close enough to the electric poles that were being put out, but our house wasn't wired to receive it. Monroe studied the situation. When he finished, lights came on and all electrical sockets worked. Except we didn't have anything to plug in!

Momma and all the girls worked for cotton farmers to earn money for a refrigerator and a freezer. Four of us, chopping for two dollars each for a twelve-hour day was a whopping eight dollars!

We would have enough money to pay down on whatever appliance was needed. The boys and Dad were raising the truck farm and digging herbs, so they would earn enough money for family food and clothing. So, all bases were covered. The family was a team.

Before harvest time, we had enough money to purchase a used Hotpoint Refrigerator in 1955 and it is still working in 2020 with no needed repairs. We also purchased a large used freezer that kept our vegetables and freed Momma from canning endlessly.

Momma was so excited. "I can make ice cream right in the freezer whenever I want!" This also meant we could have ice cream on days other than the 4th of July when we used to eat homemade custard ice cream throughout the day—one frozen large cylinder after another until we were "ice cream maxed" and happy.

You see, ice cream was my mother's favorite dessert and chewing ice from half & half coke and water was her favorite drink.

After the Fourth of July celebration that year, Momma called us together and said, "The upper elementary grades are going to be consolidated from Spring Hill Elementary to Burgess High School. That means at least three of you will have to walk one mile to the bus stop and three miles to the closest bus stop on rainy days.

I know Monroe and Jannie have finished two years at Burgess High, but Daisy ("Doll") would have to join you walking that distance. Dad and I think it might be a good time for you three to go to Piney Woods. What do you think?"

Seth Ballard, Jr., (age 21) United States Air Force

"Yes, that sounds fine, but will you have enough help with just Mamie and the two younger boys (Samuel and Sylvester)?" I asked.

"Yes, we'll be fine. With Seth, Jr.'s financial help from the Air Force, we will get along all right," assured Momma, Lucile.

- 10 -

Piney Woods School, the Family's Blessing

You cannot hold me down unless you remain
in a downward position yourself.
--Bit of Wisdom, Caring n' Sharing School

At first, my dad didn't know much about Piney Woods School. He heard that it was a good boarding school that helped predominately African-American children. He was about to learn that the school also provided a whole-life experience—educating the head, heart and hands. He learned that it was founded by Dr. Laurence C. Jones, the first African-American graduate of The University of Iowa who was divinely guided to the piney woods of Mississippi to start a school in 1909. He didn't know the school started when Dr. Jones was sitting under a cedar tree reading a paper when an African-American teenager saw him reading a paper and asked Dr. Jones to teach him how to read. Dr. Jones said yes, and the teen returned the next day with several of his friends who also wanted to learn. Thus, the simple beginning of Piney Woods School and the answer to my dad's prayer.

Dad told us the story many times. "The prophetic meeting happened one Saturday when I was dressed in a completely black Dutch suit with natural wood shoes. Dr. Laurence C. Jones was walking down Farish Street and saw me, a man of color, in this foreign outfit with bundles of herbs strung over the shoulder."

He continued: "Our eyes met—I was interested in making a sale, and Dr. Jones was interested in finding out more about me." Dad chuckled as he proceeded to tell the story.

"I introduced myself as "Herb Doctor Seth Ballard of Pocahontas, Mississippi."

"Oh, so you are an American?" asked Dr. Jones curiously.

"Yes. I dress like this because I received this suit from a Holland Seed catalog. This was my perk for making a seed order. I have been wearing it to get attention and to make herbal sales, especially, sassafras that I wear over my shoulder. It's my most popular sale!" my dad explained.

My dad, Herb Doctor Seth Ballard, of Pocahontas Mississippi. "I am the only doctor for my people, especially those who can't afford to go to or be accepted in the office of a White medical doctor."

"How did you learn about these herbs?" Dr. Jones asked.

"That's a good question. My father, Nelson, started a school up in Madison County. One day an ex-slave (called "Mr. Ex") about 103 years old stopped by with a big suitcase. He said he wanted to see what we were teaching in the school so he could teach someone about herbs. It was a new word for us, but he explained that we needed medical herbs that would grow where our people live. At that time, very few, if any, doctors treated African-American people. Mr. Ex further explained that he would like to teach me how to identify them by appearance, by smell, by taste, by the touch and general locations."

After some discussion and answering Dr. Jones' questions about being an herb doctor, Dr. Jones asked, "Do you have a family, any children?"

"Yes, I have eight children." Dad told him. The youngest is not quite one, and the oldest is fourteen."

"As your children get older, I want all of them to come to Piney Woods and I'll give them all a scholarship." Dr. Jones volunteered. With a broad smile, my dad gratefully accepted the offer and sealed it with a handshake.

(We all felt that God arranged for Dr. Jones and my dad to meet so that all the Ballard children could be educated from elementary age through junior college if we so desired. We learned to trust God for even more.)

Happenings Before and During My Experience at Piney Woods

I remember when our oldest brother, Seth went to Piney Woods Boarding School. Seth was about fourteen. About two years later, my oldest sister Rosie Mae, when she was fourteen years old, joined him. Monroe and I were the next two left in charge of the house and our younger siblings when our parents went to town. But we weren't too good at it, yet.

One day, when Monroe and I served as supervisors, Samuel decided to play on the chicken coop. He with pillow-case-cape stretched wide, took his superman plunge off the coop and sprang his wrist. The brave teen supervisors hid it for a while, but Samuel had to tell because he was in much pain. Dad didn't say much. He just beckoned for Samuel to come so he could examine the wrist for breakage. Then he went outside and created a splint from a board.

He tied it tightly so that the wrist would stay in place. Samuel seemed relieved and so were we.

Monroe and I worked together as a team because we were two years apart in age. But so were all of the eight Ballard children. We could calculate our age by subtracting or adding two to our age. Monroe and I were now the oldest in charge of the household, now in high school and went to Burgess High School in Flora.

During this time, Monroe got a job with Uncle Nathan, making concrete pipes. When that happened, I took up Monroe's chore of plowing the truck farm. I learned his job and carried it out. No problems on the farm, but there was some school news that wasn't so good.

Monroe and I were already walking at least one mile to the bus stop. Now, because the roads were too muddy for the bus to come to the bus stop on rainy days, we would have to walk another two miles to meet the bus. School consolidation also affected where Daisy went to school. She would be joining Monroe and me on the walk to the bus stop.

A difficult decision had to be made. Our parents could not fathom the idea of our getting up an hour early during inclement weather to meet the school bus. White children in public schools were picked up in front of their houses where the road was graveled, but the bus stopped at the exact point where the un-graveled road entered our neighborhood.

Dad reminded Momma that "All of the children have scholarships at Piney Woods." We can send them there instead of having them walk so far to the bus stop." He spoke. You remember that this is our blessing! This is how our children will get educated.

"Yes," responded Momma. That sounds great, but I don't think we can afford to send eight children to a boarding school."

"Oh," Dad responded, "I said the same thing. But Dr. Laurence C. Jones said he is offering a full Piney Woods scholarship to each of our eight children. We can send them as soon as we feel they are able to stay away from home and go to a boarding school. They will have chores or work assignments for part of the day and go to school at least five hours a day during the school year. However, Dr. Jones says their workdays are longer during the summer when school is out, and that's okay too. They will teach skills while teaching the whole child--using the Head, Heart and Hands."

However, I was not exactly a good fit for Piney Woods. I was used to taking responsibility and solving problems. I found it agitating to be told twice. If authority tells me twice, I get afraid, unnerved. I needed to stay at Piney Woods for the character development, but the environment was too strict. I am offended by burglar bars, for example. Piney Woods didn't have burglar bars but had many rules and people who supervised all the time. I didn't need all that.

It was good FOR me, but it was not good TO me. It helped me to be self-disciplined; I learned not to trust everybody or gossip because it will come back to you a different way.

Dad prepared us to avoid the ugliest kind of lifestyle in case we had to make a choice. He would tell me about drunkards on Farish Street (Jackson, MS) and it would make me weak in the knees with fear: "Ain't got nothing!" is what the drunkards would say after someone had taken advantage of their drunken state. Dad would stagger about dramatizing how despicable that lifestyle was without actually saying, "Don't drink."

I learned that lesson clearly and so did my siblings. So, now we had another lesson about life to remember while away from home.

The president of Piney Woods School, Dr. Laurence C. Jones, admired Dad's love for education and his dream to educate his eight children. Our dad was elated that there was a school that was considered a little town in itself. The rules were almost the same as the ones he taught his children at home—no dancing (except square dancing), no drinking or smoking by staff or students.

The school enrolled students from all ethnic groups and income levels, especially the "disadvantaged" who had promise but little or no money. (The Ballard children qualified.)

The philosophy practiced at Piney Woods was, "Come as you are." We will teach your children through the Head (intellectually), Heart (spiritually) and Hand (vocationally). The rules and routines were made clear from day one. However, I felt an excessive fear factor in the discipline method.

Since we were all born about two years apart, Dad and Momma pulled us together to explain how our family will continue being a team so all can become educated.

"Here's the way it works," Dad proceeded. Seth, Jr. was and is the overseer for Rosa Mae helping her get adjusted at Piney Woods and in life. Monroe and I paired. That's why he would later help me solve my Piney Woods maladjustment. Daisy was responsible for Mamie. Growing up, she helped Mamie adjust to first grade at Spring Hill school and was her general protector because Mamie cried easily. The final pair was Samuel and Sylvester. They were close in a lot of ways. I remember the way they would share a small box of raisins, and when counted one to one down to the last raisin, they'd cut the final raisin in half to make sure all was fair and equal.

"Now, I know if they all go to Piney Woods School and finish junior college, they can find a way to finish the last two years later; maybe each will get a scholarship. What a blessing!" Dad spoke out loud confirming his faith that God, right now, was opening up opportunities for all of their children.

"Hum, huh. Yes Lord." Momma responded as she straightened up the room where the chosen three had begun picking out their best second-hand clothes, and left rejected clothes and shoes all over the floor.

Momma submitted to the idea of sending the next three to Piney Woods.

The three were Daisy, thirteen; Monroe, seventeen and I, Jannie, fifteen. Each of us packed a seven-dollar footlocker carrying basic necessities and our prize possessions. Now, there were three left to help at home while attending Spring Hill Elementary: Mamie, eleven; Samuel, nine; and Sylvester, seven.

However, life changed for me that August afternoon in 1955 when I got off the Trailways Bus at the Piney Woods driveway on Highway 49, South of Jackson, MS. The driveway was shaped like a horseshoe with north and south entrances and exits. It was also the main street from Highway 49, through the campus and back out to Highway 49.

Carrying a foot locker, a bag of clothing and beddings with five dollars in my pocket, I walked on gravel and blacktop for the first of few times in my life. I checked into a three-story dormitory where there were city conveniences that I welcomed.

"Yes! Wow."

We didn't have a telephone at home; therefore, we communicated by "snail" mail to let everyone know I arrived safely. I also remembered what our parents had said: "Write and let us know how you are doing. Manage the money you have so it will last, about six months."

Five dollars were hard to manage for six months when we had to buy five cent-stamps to write home, and buy something for dinner every Sunday. (Piney Woods only served breakfast and lunch to students on Sundays. Dinner was on your own!)

Oddly enough, Piney Woods gave boys an allowance of seventy-five cents per week, but did not give girls any money. However, my brother and "partner," Monroe, was a giver. To help his sisters out, Monroe would cut boys' hair in the dormitory and earn extra money. Then, he gave us a quarter each to help buy food from the Canteen for the Sunday evening meal. That was great, and we were forever grateful.

I lived in Dulaney Hall, and shared a dorm room with three other girls on the second floor. I had to learn how to get along with non-relatives without parental supervision. However, we always had a matron on the first floor near the front door. Ms Gant was also the school counselor and school nurse. She was introduced to us as one of the first African-American registered nurses in Mississippi, but many of us questioned that.

Ms Gant thought a dose of Castor oil was the cure for whatever ailed us. In a way it was because we'd rather claim to be well than to take a big dose of Castor oil.

At Piney Woods, we had few to no fights in our dormitory. We had close supervision day and night, but some girls still got away with mischief. The girls timed the night guards' rounds on our end of the campus. Then they would tie sheets together to get down from the second floor. They met with the boys behind the dorm and returned without getting caught.

The renegades had the help of schoolmates who held the sheets to let them down and to pull them back up after their escapade. The timing was crucial, cooperation was key, secrecy was important too. They risked expulsion to do what they wanted. I couldn't take that chance. I watched sometimes, but remembered I had to keep my Ballard reputation that my older siblings had established.

My peers took "social chances" that could outweigh the temporary, consequential rewards. I didn't allow the "drives of nature" or commitment to friends to urge me to do the unthinkable. I learned I should beware of those who try to change my sound moral values. I decided to be a leader, to influence *their* minds to *do right and go straight.*

The following year, after much persuading, Mamie, age twelve, was given the chance to go to Piney Woods. Being without her best friend and partner, Daisy, had not been easy. So, when Momma said she could go, she gladly packed her precious belongings in the biggest used suitcase available, bundled her beddings that were required to bring and made ready to attend Piney Woods.

Arriving on the bus at the Piney Woods entrance, Mamie struggled to carry her bags to the dormitory. Momma could not help much because she was recuperating from a back injury. Some Piney Woods boys saw her struggling and came to help her to the dorm. Mamie was so glad and even happier when she discovered she was placed in the same room with her sisters, Daisy and me. The transition from home was not hard for this five-feet, six-inch twelve-year-old girl. In fact, she said it was one of the happiest days of her life.

By now, Seth had graduated from Piney Woods Junior College and joined the Air Force. He was sending a support check home every month to help. Seth bought the first family car in 1958. It was a 1952 Chevrolet Sedan!

Now, Momma and Daddy could pick up the Ballard bunch from Piney Woods instead of finding someone with a car to do that. For the first time, we had a car!

Samuel and Sylvester stayed together until Momma and Dad decided to send Samuel to Piney Woods in 1962. That was a tough separation for the final two. Sylvester was lonely, but was a child of faith. He prayed and read the Bible a lot to help fill the void. He prayed for his siblings who were away in school. Then, he said something supernatural happened. He was led to a spot under an oak tree behind our house. There he said an angel wrote a message on the ground in what appeared to be another language. A few of us saw it. One was my sister Mamie who witnessed the code writing on the ground, but could not decipher it. The message stayed for weeks undisturbed in the dirt under the oak tree. Sylvester, about age ten, knew what the message revealed about life at Piney Woods, but just told us what was relevant to us individually.

Rosie Mae was still at Piney Woods when Daisy, Monroe and I arrived. Rosa was in the college dorm for upper-class students. Rosa worked four hours a day in the President's home as a cook when she wasn't in class. Everyone said she was a good worker. Several years later, her good behavior and excellent work ethics caused her to be awarded a scholarship to Alcorn College to complete her college degree.

Prior to the Air Force, Seth, Jr. had also been awarded a two-year scholarship from Piney Woods to attend Alcorn College where he was to complete his final two years of college. The two oldest children had set the standards high for the Ballard children. My dad's prophetic statement at Seth, Jr.'s birth was that he would attend Alcorn College, the first land grant college for African Americans in Mississippi. Not only did Seth, Jr. attend, but Rosa did too.

My Piney Woods Experience

I would say that my experiences at Piney Woods were both positive and negative. It freed me from the long country mile walks to the New Spring Hill School (1950--1953), from cotton fields, dusty and muddy roads, from the wood-burning heaters and cooking stove, from the outhouses, no running water, no electricity, and long walks to the bus stop. Piney Woods would save me from the long bus rides to Burgess High School in Flora, MS (1953--1955).

Going to Piney Woods would be an introduction to running water, indoor toilets, radiator heat, electric lights and dormitory life in (three levels) basement, ground floor and upstairs. The student-made bricks that formed the gray brick buildings usually had student activity centers in basements. This was all good.

However, my unfavorable experience was not direct but a byproduct because of the kind of person I have always been. I've always been sensitive, quick to hear and ready to keep rules and regulations. Concerning behavior and consequences, I never wanted to get punished for making foolish choices, doing outlandish stuff, showing disrespect for authority, testing the rules or the patience or in-charge persons or failing to do my school work and chores. I was a working student, that meant I worked a half-day and went to school a half day.

Work assignments were assigned based on experience, general aptitude or age. The older trained students would count the financial donations to Piney Woods and classify cash by denominations. Checks would be placed in a separate box, endorsed and counted for deposit. These checkers were high school and junior college students who had been trained by the "Dean of Everything," Mrs. Eula Kelly Moman, who also served as the comptroller.

Donations by the sacksful were coming in response to the recent appeal on "This Is Your Life," a program that featured the founder, Dr. Laurence C. Jones, his loyal staff, the beginning stages and struggles of Piney Woods School. It provided a real financial boost for Piney Woods, raising a total of $1,117,000 to establish an endowment to ensure the school remains open and viable for predominately African-American promising students. In the late 1950s, $1,117,000 (one million one hundred seventeen thousand dollars) was a lot of money for a historically African-American boarding school in Mississippi.

The Dean supervised the incoming mail, directing students to use the letter opener to open the mail and place donations in big boxes. Those would be moved to the team that would take out cash or checks and stack each in assigned boxes. The money was then counted by trained and trusted junior college students before turning the assorted funds to Mrs. Eula Kelly Moman, the comptroller.

My job was to write "thank you" letters to donors. During my afternoon work hours, I also learned shorthand. In late evening, I also learned to play the trombone in the school band. I was doing my work and participating in extracurricular activities. Yet, I felt nervous all the time. I was afraid I would get into trouble.

Mrs. Eula Kelly Moman was an in-charge person at Piney Woods. She was in charge of most departments and controlled the decisions about everything that occurred on the campus. Mrs. Moman was the power to be reckoned with. The very sight of her gave me chills to my bones--exciting fear from my head to my toes! The sound of her high shrilling, piercing voice gave me headaches, every day, all day!

I never had conversations with Mrs. Moman. But it didn't matter whether she said, "Good Morning" or something complimentary, it never brought a smile to my face or made me feel good because I was afraid of her.

Although she was a powerful person and made things happen at Piney Woods, I cannot say what lessons I learned from her or from this experience. As a sensitive person, I didn't need her bigger-than-life attitude--the fear she engendered to make one respect and obey her instructions. Therefore, the headaches kept coming every day. I had no formal medical knowledge but I knew nothing good could result from my daily headaches.

So, I decided I would write a letter to Aunt Bessie because I heard Momma say she asked if I could come stay with her. I told Aunt Bessie I was finishing twelfth grade and would love to come live with her.

Subsequently, I asked my mother and father to allow me to go to St. Louis, MO to live with my Aunt Bessie Ballard Rozelle after high school and go to college there. Since Aunt Bessie had already expressed a desire for me to live with her in St. Louis, it was great timing. She promised my parents that she would be completely responsible for all my needs including sending me to college.

I had learned that all adults are not caring and some cannot be trusted. That is what my parents were toying with. They didn't know whether going to St. Louis would be better than Piney Woods. And, more importantly, it may be a disappointment.

My Brother Monroe to the Rescue

My dad was afraid I would lose my part-time work scholarship at Piney Woods. He doubted whether Aunt Bessie, a widow woman, could keep her promise long term. I wasn't able to persuade Dad. Therefore, I asked Monroe, my brother, my assigned partner, to meet Dad in Jackson and plead my case. He did and was able to convince Dad to let me go to St. Louis. As my partner, Monroe felt compelled to think of a way to persuade Dad to let me go to St. Louis, and he was successful. So, my parents' "pair-partner" idea in the family of eight children worked quite well.

I washed off and packed my Piney Woods-used footlocker in preparation to leave Piney Woods, Mississippi and go to St. Louis, Missouri.

I will always be grateful to the Piney Woods School and the Piney Woods staff for being my bridge over and the tunnel through troubled waters. I learned, initially, that there was no good or value in the *fear* I experienced at Piney Woods. But later, I learned that fear is the absence of faith. I was young so I hadn't learned that yet, but I knew something was missing. The PW experience taught me about life in a way that nothing else would have taught me.

After finishing twelfth grade at Piney Woods, I went to St. Louis, MO, a big urban city, to attend Harris-Stowe University. I was SO afraid, but I believed I could make it because Piney Woods had prepared me with the basic skills in urban living and urban survival.

My going north (Missouri for me) was a common practice for African Americans to go north for higher education or for jobs. In the 1950s African- Americans couldn't go to any university. High school graduates had to attend the underfunded historically African-American colleges—currently referred to as the Historically Black Colleges and Universities (HBCU's). However, my motivation was a little different in that I went north to escape Mrs. Moman as well as to attend college. I left Mississippi at age seventeen and I stayed for seventeen years.

Jannie, Age Seventeen

I saw the importance and power in saying what you mean and meaning what you say. I learned it was important to be consistent in dealings so those who work with, or for you, will know what to do and what to expect. Now in St. Louis, Aunt Bessie was a blessing to me, an emotional life safer; a promise keeper. Today, I learned to *play it forward* at the Caring n' Sharing School where we help steer students who were like me--needing understanding and direction.

- 11 -

Transitioning from Mississippi to Missouri

You can go farther and faster if you avoid racial prejudices.
--From "Bits of Wisdom," Caring n' Sharing School

I left Piney Woods and arrived in St. Louis on the Trail Ways Bus. My dad's sister, Aunt Bessie Ballard Rozelle met me at the bus station and took me to her brick house. I discovered that I was the only child there. All Aunt Bessie's children were grown and independent with families. Therefore, I had my own room. At age seventeen, it was a new and welcomed experience. During that time, she also purchased new clothes for me and helped me enroll in college as she had promised. "Wow! I'm blessed." I thought thankfully.

After enrolling at Harris Teacher's College, I immediately noticed a racial difference from the college experiences I would have had in Mississippi. In 1957, it was the beginning of desegregation in St. Louis, but in Mississippi racial unrest had just begun with sit-ins, boycotts and marches. No institutions were integrated until 1962 when James Meredith became the first African-American student admitted to the segregated University of Mississippi. At Harris Teacher's College, I had majority white classmates and majority white teachers. Therefore, I felt compelled to study hard so I would not embarrass my parents or Aunt Bessie who was investing in me.

Aunt Bessie not only kept her promise to send me to college, but she also defrayed all related expenses without complaining.

During my second year of college, I came home wearing glasses. Dad poked fun at me, but it didn't hurt me enough to change my self-esteem. It didn't cause me to be revengeful or respond disrespectfully to him. I learned early that other people cannot dictate my destiny or my emotions. I did not think less of myself, less of my father or of my giving up. However, I do remember the unwelcomed feelings.

I returned to St. Louis. I made it through college and received my diploma with a lifetime license to teach in Missouri. My first attempt taking the National Teachers Exam and getting a passing score was successful. I was graduated on time with a Bachelor of Arts degree in Education and Psychology (Grades K-nineth) in 1962.

Jannie's College Graduation - 1962

Aunt Bessie Ballard Rozelle, was good *to* me and St. Louis was good *for* me. Unlike home in Mississippi, I lived in a house with running water, electricity and store-bought food that I had seen very little of except on special occasions. Aunt Bessie took me to her church, Christ Temple Church of Christ Holiness at 4301 Page Boulevard, pastored by Bishop A. Dewey Williams.

I was not used to attending church every Sunday or having transportation to attend more than once a month. In Mississippi, Uncle Nathan Wiggins (Aunt Mamie's husband) picked us up the first Sunday of each month for church. Of course, all eight of us plus Dad and Momma could not fit in Uncle Nathan's six-seater Plymouth car. Therefore, our parents would attend monthly, but the children would attend, four per Sunday, on alternate months. The maximum attendance for the children would be six times out of a year. As said earlier, when weather was bad, we had church at home with Dad and Momma officiating. That part was good.

Full Time Service for A Full Time God

My new church was open every day of the week. We had Sunday school and church services, youth meetings, men's meetings, women's meetings, auxiliaries' meetings, Boy Scouts and Girl Scouts, choir rehearsals, business meetings, fellowship dinners, visiting ministers or missionaries, special programs, weddings, funerals or some other activities from Sunday through Saturday. We were held accountable for being present and always prepared. We never, never cancelled scheduled services for any unscheduled activity. Our church was an organized church with leaders who were always prepared to serve.

I Thank God for the Memories

We, the youngsters, enjoyed church. We walked to church day and night; we had no cars or mobile phones. We enjoyed walking and talking. We liked going to choir rehearsal because the boys and girls had "eyes" for each other. Most of us married fellow choir members (non-relative of course) after college or vocational school. Our choir director, Mrs. Lelia M. Thompson, coordinated and directed our weddings. (We all got married in a span of two-years.)

Today, with a grateful heart, I look back and I remember those who loved me first and who taught me how to live and how to stay out of trouble. I did not see but they had vision for me. They took on the responsibility to make clear the distinction between right and wrong, good and evil. They made me listen attentively and then held me accountable.

So that I wouldn't forget them, I have listed those who loved me and taught me and my peers the way to live in this present world and to be prepared for the hereafter. First, Pastor/Bishop A. Dewey Williams and Assistant Pastor Elder Hugh Jarmon worked together to preach God's word in a way that all of us got his or her personal message. The Sunday School Supt. Sandford E. Bell, Assist. Supt. Julius Collins, and Secretary Geraldine B. Moore worked together to make Sunday School exciting and sometimes competitive, especially for the younger members. The Adult Women Sunday school class was facilitated by Sis. Louise Bell. These church leaders also worked cooperatively with Youth Leaders, Sis. Lelia Mae Thompson and Little Lelia Mae Thompson. The Children and Junior Choirs were also led by Sis. Lelia Thompson with Sisters Virgina Jarmon and Ruby Martin. The Gospel Chorus was conducted by Sis. Nellie Curry and the Senior Choir by Sis. Amelia Bell. The Adult Ushers' group was led by Sis. Elgy Bagsy and the Junior Ushers were supervised by Sis. Panzie Burris. Sis. Hattie Brown held the Girl Scouts meetings and Bro. Richard Buie managed the Boy Scouts. Young Ladies' ministry was sponsored by Sis. Myrtle P. Fairbanks. The Children's ministry and dramatic presentations were created and directed by my Aunt Bessie Ballard Rozelle (for thirty-four years).

Other ministries that set the religious atmosphere were the Brotherhood ministry headed by Bro. Richard Buie and Bro. Robert Bruce. The Chairman of the Deacon board was also a State Representative, Bro. Fred E. Brown, who led eleven deacons in various church ministries. Chairmen of the Trustee Board were Bro. Robert White and Bro. Robert Bruce. Sisters Annie Irving and Carmet Hill led the adult Sisters' Ministries. Music for all occasions was conducted by Sis. Lelia M. Thompson, Sis. Amelia Bell, Sis. Barbara F. Carter and Sis. Nellie Curry. Weddings, programs and plays were conducted by Sisters Lelia Thompson, and Bessie B. Rozelle. Sis. Viola Johnson, my mother-in-law, led the noon-day prayer. For all of them, I thank God, but I still had more to learn about life in St. Louis. That comes next.

Everything that is legal or lawful, is not always Christian or right.
--From "Bits of Wisdom," Caring n' Sharing School

- 12 -

More of the St. Louis Experience

Before you talk, give it thought.
--From "Bits of Wisdom," Caring n' Sharing School

As introduced earlier, I had a teaching-preaching pastor, Bishop A. Dewey Williams at Christ Temple Church of Christ Holiness (USA) at 4301 Page Blvd. Bishop Williams was a self-taught scholar; he had himself together as a person, husband, father and pastor. He and his wife Lillian had two daughters and one son. Their children represented them well, too. This was what I expected, and I delighted in seeing what a Christian family looked like.

I remember what I saw and I remember what I heard.

Bishop Williams often quoted the scripture, Hosea 4:6: "My people are destroyed for lack of knowledge ..." It was his determination that his congregation would not be destroyed for lack of knowledge. He used the KJV Bible as his source for defining right and wrong; determining what's moral and what's immoral; proper and improper behavior. He made clear the distinctions between male and female and the behavior of the single and the married folks.

Bishop Williams and his ready-and-abled staff discipled us as if we were their total responsibility. They were not a paid staff; only about five of them got any kind of compensation. They taught the core, basics and fundamentals of life. They made me to know that behavior is not a racial thing but a personal choice. Injustice is not a virtue; neither is it an excuse for revenge. I needed to know that for my personal maturity.

The old folks at this church talked about lazy folks and the "won't-work folks." They had no sympathy for the loafers, the free riders or tax burdens. They had a scripture for them that stated: ... "If any would not work, neither should he EAT" (II Thessalonian 3:10).

The church leaders identified sinful, shameful and disgraceful behavior as: fornication and adultery; drinking and using drugs; gambling and lying; cheating and stealing; killing, violence and abuse of any kind. Incest, nudity and pornography were not to be practiced or heard about among us according to the scriptures (I Cor. 6:9-11, KJV).

Therefore, we youngsters did not have to guess at what was right or wrong. We did not have to figure out how to determine who was a good person or a bad person. All of that was defined and described for us with gusto and passion. I don't remember who told us that sex outside of marriage is a sin before God. But now, I know that teaching came from the scriptures: "Flee fornication. Every sin that a man doeth is without the body; but he that committeth fornication sinneth against his own body" (I Cor. 6:18, KJV).

So, to have sex or NOT to have sex was NEVER the question of age or the seriousness of a relationship. The question was always, "Are you married or not?" Therefore, single boys, girls and unmarried adults are to abstain.

Although it is a tradition, it is also good etiquette for a girl to follow a wholesome image. If she chose to be sexually active or have a baby out of wedlock, she should not wear a white dress or cover her face with a veil at her wedding. To do so would disrespect the principle of purity that the white dress represented, and the veil that indicated the girl's innocence. THAT, in my opinion, WAS AND IS THE TRADITIONAL PIVOT OF MORALITY!

My church at 4301 Page Blvd, St. Louis where I was married, 1962

At church, I attended most of the activities. During these socials, I met my would-be husband, Lem Johnson. Our puritanical relationship grew. He respected me and I did my best to respect and not entice him. However, my nylon dress with embroidered trees may have challenged his Christian thoughts. He said that the Spirit told him that I would be his wife. At that time, God had not spoken to me. But later God impressed me that he was the one.

Mr. & Mrs. Lem Johnson

Lem and I married on June 24, 1962. Momma, Dad and Mamie (my baby sister) came on the bus from Jackson, MS to attend the wedding. The family members in St. Louis assigned different ones to car pool so that we could accommodate out-of-town guests.

On my special day, everyone arrived in time for the wedding except Mamie. She was assigned to ride with Geraldine, a first cousin who was customarily late, but Mamie didn't know it. This day was no exception for Geraldine. The two arrived at the end of the wedding when Lem and I were coming down the tall stairs at the entrance of the church and rice was being thrown.

I tell this part of the story because it was so dramatic. Mamie burst into tears and could not stop crying. People looked at her with questionable disdain, thinking silently: "Crying at a wedding is not quite that serious! Right?" Mamie felt she had traveled by bus from Mississippi for the wedding, and missed the ceremony!

'What will I say to family when I return home? Oh yes, I went to Jannie's wedding but missed it. What kind of sense does that make?" Mamie pondered over and over while tears kept falling.

Being a natural crier, Mamie could not stop crying long enough to take a decent wedding picture. I don't think I have a single wedding picture with Mamie in it. It's like she was never there. That is another reason she said she couldn't stop crying. Even years later, she would tear up when talking about it.

Other than that mishap, it was a beautiful wedding.

Lem and I rented a three-room upstairs apartment with living room, bedroom, kitchen, bath and back porch. It was nice and safe.

In 1968, we bought our first home at 7114 Lexington Avenue, Velda Village, MO 63121 (Metro St. Louis, MO). The monthly note was $107.00 for a unique brick house on a one-half acre lot. If it were not an acre, it looked like it was. Its backyard had a back gate that let into a big parking lot of a church that gave us extra viewing. We enjoyed and thought it was beautiful.

Now, we wanted a child. Nothing was happening. We thought if I stopped working and rested more, I would get pregnant. After praying and hoping for several years, it still didn't happen. So, I enrolled in Missouri University, Normandy, MO to work on a Master's degree in counseling.

The curriculum was very disappointing. I wanted to learn how to help children. That didn't happen. I withdrew from that program and enrolled in an adult night school at Normandy High. I took Auto Mechanics. The first semester was Motor and second semester was General Mechanics of an automobile.

In the second year, I studied Creative Writing, and decided to return to my first love, teaching.

After applying for a teaching position, I was hired to teach first grade at McKinley Elementary on Lucas-Hunt Road, Velda Village, MO-- a county school. No references were necessary. I team-taught with Mrs. Margie Allen. She was married to Charles and they had two daughters. I saw how precious a family with children seemed to be and that made me want a child even more.

I returned to teaching in the Fall of 1970, and got pregnant January of 1971. I finished that year and took a three-year maternity leave. After a while, I chose to terminate my teaching career in preparation for motherhood.

After our son, Lemzel, was born, Momma came up from Mississippi to stay with me the first two weeks after my leaving the hospital. I needed that because I was so afraid of caring for a little helpless baby who totally depended on me.

I chose to breast feed. "Ouch, ouch!" It was painful at first, but I did it for about ten months. Breast feeding did prove to be convenient and very healthy for Lemzel.

My husband, Lem Johnson, was working at General Motors on Union Boulevard and Natural Bridge. One day, in late January, he came home and said his job was cutting back and laying off workers with less than ten years of seniority. My husband had nine and one-half years. Therefore, he was laid off.

This was a good job with good pay, benefits, healthcare and vacations. General Motors promised severance pay and benefits for a year. So, my husband said, "Let's move back to Mississippi during this year."

I didn't want to make such a decision, but knew something

drastic had to happen now that we were new parents. At this time, we needed a good job more than ever.

I did not want to go through a long, drawn out process trying to sell our home. I wanted the new owners to love our place and take care of it. I didn't want it torn up by a family with a bunch of unruly children.

In the window of time between being laid off and our moving, Lem got a part-time job at the public library about eight blocks from our home on Natural Bridge Road. He took a homemade "For Sale" sign to the library and posted it on the bulletin board.

Within a week, two couples came by to look at our house. The second couple bought it and told us we had a place to stay any time we came back to St. Louis. They had one son, and so did we.

We sold the house in late spring of 1974 to Mr. & Mrs. Willie Stringer. We had to be out by July first. The night of June thirtieth, we slept on the floor because we had everything packed in the U-Hall and car for an early morning departure from St. Louis.

The three of us loaded up for the trip to Mississippi. Lemzel was almost three.

During the first years after relocating, we went back to see the Stringers who now lived in our first house. The couple had made a few modifications to the house, but they all looked great. The Stringers renewed their invitation for us to visit any time we were in St. Louis. They were good people and kind. We considered visiting, maybe, but felt no need to go back to check on the house.

- 13 -

Returning to Mississippi

There comes a time in one's life when
needs and curiosities are not
as great, and desires are not as many.
--- Jannie Johnson

Our son, Lemzel, was two-and-a- half when we left St. Louis in 1974. We had all our stuff, important items with us. We sold some and gave away some. We left St. Louis early July 2, 1974 and got to Mississippi before dark. Momma Lucile Ballard, had the family men waiting to welcome us at 927 Robinson Springs Road, Madison and to help us unload initial items for immediate use.

Before leaving St. Louis, we had sent $300 to Momma for her to get Mr. John Porter to build or extend a room on the "fruit house" (a place family kept canned vegetables and fruits especially for winter). It now would be used to store our things until we built a house.

When my younger sister Mamie learned that we were returning to Mississippi to stay, she immediately thought of ways to support the transition.

She and husband, Walter, had a son, Walter, Jr. who was a little more than a year old. They had hired Aunt Lillie Palmer as a nanny for him while both went to work at Jackson State University. Considering the win-win situation with little Walter, Jr. having a playmate with Lemzel at two-and-a-half they decided to hire Jannie at the end of the school year. That worked out fine until a greater idea was born. Mamie decided that the environment created for Walter, Jr. and Lemzel was the kind that all parents needed.

In the fall of 1974, the Crocketts' family room was transformed into a kindergarten setting. It wasn't hard for my sister Mamie who was one of the first in Mississippi to get a degree in Early Childhood Education with emphasis in Montessori. As Co-Director for the Early Childhood Center at JSU, she loved creating environments for children. Other parents heard about the little private school and wanted their children to attend. Mamie also discovered in her current teaching of kindergarteners that a need existed beyond the intellectual development, etc. She wanted to add a Bible principle-based-character development piece to this pilot curriculum that was not allowable in a public university. Her Christian-principled character development piece would infuse the curriculum for the pre-school academic lessons she envisioned. Mamie asked me to help develop the character development lessons for the curriculum.

By 1975, the Crockett's family room became increasingly crowded as the clientele grew with me as the primary teacher. Therefore, Mamie and Walter Crockett founded The Learning Tree Child Development Center and moved the enrollees and me to a new location on Sivley Avenue in Jackson. I became the Character Development teacher at the Learning Tree. My job was to build child-friendly stories and/or scenarios based on the principle of the memory verse that Mamie selected. Sometimes she would also create a tune and use puppets so children could more quickly memorize the verses that went with the creative lessons. This teaching position occurred during my first year back in Mississippi.

My brother-in-law, Sam Cobbins (Daisy's husband) personally took responsibility for preparing a place for us to stay. He remodeled my dad's Herb Office to accommodate us. We stayed there from 1974 until it burned in 1977.

It was sometime in January 1977 that an electrical problem appeared to have caused the fire. That day, I was at my sister Daisy's house teaching a group of youngsters. Momma, called and said, "Your house is on fire!" Those words were ones that no one ever wants to hear. I rushed from Jackson, about ten miles away, to get there in time to save some of our possessions. I arrived about the same time as the firemen.

The house was fully engulfed when firemen got there. We witnessed the walls falling inward. Firemen from Madison, about five miles away, used the tank of water they brought, putting out most of the fire, but saving nothing. No vital records of birth certificates, degrees, bank account records or family pictures were saved. To ensure that the fire didn't spread to Momma's house about 500 feet away, firemen and everyone drew water from a nearby pond to weaken the strongest flames.

Lem, my husband, had gone to the woods to cut and bring wood to fuel the wood-burning kitchen stove and bedroom heater. On his way home, he decided to stop by the pasture to feed the cows. A neighbor saw him and stopped to say, "Man your house is on fire!"

He couldn't believe this because he had just left about an hour earlier. He was babysitting Lemzel, our son, who was asleep in the house. Lem said he thought about leaving him since he was coming right back. But the Holy Spirit reminded him of the old saying: "Never leave a sleeping child alone in a house." So, fortunately, he bundled Lemzel up, loaded him carefully in the back seat of his truck and carried him along while doing his errands in the winter cold. Lem and I were so grateful that Lemzel was unharmed and alive that the loss of other possessions didn't pain as much.

My husband asked Momma, again, if we could stay with her until we could regroup. She, of course, said yes.

"You all may have Dad's room in the back," Momma offered. We call the back-bedroom Dad's room because he died there in 1973.

Momma did not charge rent. She just asked us to share the cost of food and expenses of any long-distance calls. She was considerate and loyal. However, she did NOT allow our dog, Lexis, in the house or in her yard. Lexis was trained to obey our voice commands, but could be vicious and even dangerous to strangers. Therefore, we conformed to her wishes.

Our family of three stayed with Momma at 927 Robinson Springs Road, Madison, MS until October 1977.

Sam Cobbins, my brother-in-law, again took up the responsibility of helping us relocate. He, with a few student volunteers from Jackson State University, built us a three-bed-room home with a small kitchen and one and one-half bathroom from ground up for $1,000 plus cost of materials. Knowing our great loss of everything, he gave us ten months to pay it off. But we chose to pay it off earlier--never missing a month's payment.

Sam Cobbins built our house on the ten acres of land we had recently bought from a neighbor, Mr. Clarence Taylor and his mother Mrs. Etta Webster. We paid cash for the ten acres at $1,000 per acre. He told us that we could buy as many acres as we wanted, and select any location we wanted. He was selling it all because his mother, Mrs. Webster was no longer able to farm it. Mr. Clarence Taylor had his own property up near Mt. Center Church in Pocahontas, MS, about three miles away from his mother's house.

Mrs. Webster was our neighbor, a good, dependable neighbor. I remember that she had an electric refrigerator before the Ballard family did. She used extra ice trays to make ice for us. Someone from our house would go to her house and pick up the ice every other day or so. Wow! That was great, especially in the hot Mississippi summers.

It was a common practice for neighbors to do for each other without thought of labor involved or cost. Doing good deeds for each other made survival possible for us in south Madison County Mississippi.

I have learned that life will sometimes throw a curve ball. It looks straight, but it curves unexpectantly and causes you to miss. During these trials, I recalled a lesson on "Quitting" that I taught to a youth group.

"You've done your best. You've tried to understand and be understanding. You've even gone the extra mile. You are willing to forgive and forget. But nothing, just nothing, seems to be working out for long. If it's not this; it's that, but always *something*. In fact, the thought of quitting sometimes knocks at your mind's door. It's a battle. You're almost persuaded because from a reasoning point of view quitting makes more sense. But you thank God for His word; the Holy scriptures: Philippians 4:13 "I can do all things through Christ which strengthens me." And 1 John 4:4 …" greater is he that is in you, than he that is in the world." Then, you shake your head as if you've just received a blow to the head, and say like the engine in *Little Red Engine*, "I think I can, I think I can" and renew the fight with life again.

Re-Establishing in Mississippi

In the late 1970s, I had a condition in my body that caused me great concern for my life. I was a young wife with a three-year old son. I was afraid. I wanted to live. I went to the home of Missionary Sis. Emma Carpenter-Bearden. She took me into her prayer room. It was an inner room in the center of her home. Everything in that room was white and there were no windows. Sis. Bearden read the Bible, prayed and prayed and then she sang Bishop Jones' songs. The song that I took home with me that day was, "O Soul Beset," (*His Fullness Hymnbook, p. 151*). She slowly sang every verse. The words ministered to my fearful and doubting heart.

I left her home with verses four and five in my heart and in my spirit. Verse four states: "O let not Satan frighten thee, Trust God and His salvation see, He will not fail thee, trust Him still, He every promise will fulfil. Verse five states: He loves thy faith in Him to try; But if thou trust thou shalt not die; He'll roll the roaring sea away. He'll turn the darkest night to day."

I continued to work at the Learning Tree with my sister Mamie, Director. However, through the physical pain and feeding on the Word, I began to see a broader picture. God was directing me to do more.

I checked with a large school district to see if they could use a teacher who could come in periodically and teach children how to "Do right, and go straight." I could possibly, work with their Drug Free Initiative and help to reduce the number of disciplinary referrals during the regular school day. The response finally came.

By the school year 1989--1999, I was working with eleven elementary schools in a large urban school district reaching over 30,000 students annually. Principals reported 80 to 95% reduction in disciplinary referrals. That was a sign that I was on the right track.

Our son, Lemzel, was now in elementary school. I also wanted to spend more time with him while helping others. However, attending the Madison schools was a challenge for Lemzel. Teachers assigned mountains of homework and I had to teach along with his teachers. I visited the school during the day just to see how the educational climate was in this predominately White elementary school.

Nevertheless, being a full-time mother with a flexible work schedule was not enough. Lemzel was assessed and recommended to repeat the second grade. I was devastated and crushed.

"Here I am a certified teacher and my child is struggling to learn and keep up," was the refrain I wrestled with in my mind. I cried for three days! Then, my husband and I went to confer with the teachers about our options. The officials said we had the option to sign for Lemzel to move to the third grade, or remain in second grade as recommended. We asked our eight-year-old son to advise us from his viewpoint. He said, "I'd rather repeat second grade than to go to third grade and have to work extra hard to prove myself. I believe I can make up the grade later."

And that is what he did while in college when going to Tougaloo College. With the support of my husband, Lem, through the years, Lemzel has become a successful author and head of a *busy* family with a wife and four children.

At this writing, I am doing well at eighty-plus years. I am a witness to the words of Bishop Charles Price Jones, "*Trust God, be still and know that He is God.*" Blessings will come as life goes on; so will challenges.

Lemzel and family left Oklahoma where they had been called to minister in a small multi-cultural community still racially in transition. His young family had to adjust to a spiritually draining and socially deleterious environment.

Left to right: Lemzel, Jr., Zarya, Zavier, Trizel, Trinita (wife) and Lemzel

After the fourth child was born in Oklahoma, it was clear that this environment would not be good for his young family to continue there. Being our only child, his circumstances affected ours. My husband and I were supportive of his decision to return closer home. With three years of experience behind them, this young family moved on to Memphis.

Lemzel was led to resume a ministry with the Neighborhood Christian Center in Memphis where his Uncle Monroe and Aunt JoeAnn Ballard conduct a multi-state compassionate ministry. It was a different position from the one in Decatur, Alabama where he previously served as a Neighborhood Christian Center Director.

Now, in a safer environment, he resumed a similar compassionate ministry on a larger scale, dealing with a multi-cultural population on different levels ranging from drug abuse, poverty and illiteracy to homelessness. The challenges were great but doable.

Shortly after being in Memphis, Lemzel was diagnosed with a tumor in the lower cavity of his skull the size of a baseball. It caused seizures and limited mobility. He was prohibited from driving; therefore, some of his responsibilities at NCC were limited. He could not drive himself to work. The family was literally grounded. Trinita, his wife, began homeschooling their two children of school age as well as caring for the two younger ones and husband.

During the initial seizure, my husband and I left Jackson to support the family and pray for healing. Simultaneously, my sister Daisy was hospitalized in Jackson also fighting for her life at St. Dominic's Hospital. My family decided to hold the announcement that Daisy passed while I was in route to Memphis.

We were not ready for Daisy to leave us the day she died. But after learning of her private trips to the doctor, final diagnoses and personal desire to inform very few of her serious illness, we understood. Being the primary caregiver for our mother until she passed as well as "nurse" for in-laws who lived with her during recuperation, she, unselfishly, said she did not want to impose on others during her illness. Daisy, therefore, prayed for a short illness and God granted the desires of her heart. Daisy did not survive her complicated diagnoses and passed in March of 2008.

Daisy was the second sibling to pass within a year. Our oldest sister went to be with the Lord in October 2007, a few days before her seventieth birthday on October 20. Then, the grief compounded when my brother Monroe, who was struggling with prostate cancer, passed one month after Daisy in April 2008. The following year, August 2009, we experienced the sudden death of our oldest sibling, Seth, Jr. Unfortunately, within two years, four of my siblings passed. Four, of course, were left to finish our divine purposes. The surviving four gather, periodically, to help maintain the old home place where I still conduct the Caring n' Sharing School.

Left to right: Samuel Ballard, Jannie B. Johnson,
Mamie B. Crockett and Sylvester Ballard,
the surviving four (2010)

I have learned to believe in His divine power. He has turned my night to day several times. I can say with confidence, no matter how dark and hopeless one's case or situation might seem, choose to trust God, re-gard-less. He will every promise fulfill.

Our son, Lemzel, still deals with some health issues, but generally he has defied all medical predictions and diagnoses. He is very much alive, drives and travels across the country speaking on *Life Lessons* from his books and as a motivational speaker for business leaders and church groups.

Elder Lem Johnson and Jannie Johnson (back row)
Students of Caring n' Sharing School who have completed 45
consecutive hours of Preventive Counseling (front row)

- 14 -

Caring n' Sharing School: Radio and Television Teachings

To change from good to evil is not wise, but to
change from evil to good is noble.
–From "Bits of Wisdom," Caring n' Sharing School

I share in this section My Truth Message that my students grow on along with my mantra on Trusting God with Tenets that also helped me along the way.

The primary part of this section will quote *Teachings and Lessons for Life* that are shared to highlight how I "coach" children who need guidance through turbulent times in their lives. To reach a larger audience, several teachings and life lessons are shared through the media of Radio and Television. Also, life lessons and coping skills are taught in small groups at the Caring n' Sharing School of Preventive Counseling on Thursday evenings, 6 PM to 8 PM, and on Saturday mornings from 9 AM to 12 Noon. Using a strategic telephone call, I encourage and monitor middle and high school students who have been truant, habitually tardy for school or for cutting class.

I have video testimonials of parents and teachers who state that these teachings and strategies have improved the children's social behavior, have considerably decreased the number of high school dropouts at respective schools, as well as inspired many to attend college and choose professional careers.

Letters to *Precious Ones* and family members are written to address concerns of parents and grandparents across various school districts who could not always bring their children to the weekend classes for small group interactive instruction that is designed to build self-esteem and purpose in a positive responsive environment.

Jannie Johnson's "My Truth Message"

1. The **truth** must be spoken to be heard. The truth must be written to be read. The truth must be shown to be seen.
2. **Truth** goes where it is invited; stays where it is respected and blesses where it is known and practiced.
3. Without the truth, solutions cannot be found.
4. Knowing how to live is just as important as knowing how to make a living.
5. Experience is NOT always the best teacher and bought sense is NOT always affordable.

On Trusting God

I have taught many lessons on "trusting God" and "thinking before you act." But before I could teach, there were a few rules of life I had to learn. Below are some of those tenets that helped me do better what I do today. TENETS (Common Sense Guard Rails) in life help us avoid pitfalls and hardships. My goal is to inform as many as will listen, but first I learned to listen.

Now, I will share tenets that helped me become the person, wife, parent, child of God and teacher I am today. Herein are "Tenets," Guideposts and Lessons I learned and have practiced to the best of my ability.

Tenets That Helped Me Along Life's Journey

1. Herb Dr. Seth Ballard, my dad, said: "If parents do right and go straight, their children will *mighty-near* do the same."
2. Lucile Palmer Ballard, my mother said: "Let your head rule your body not your body, (passion/urges) rule your head." Pregnancy is not a disease you catch. It's the result of a particular behavior.
3. "If and when you have a problem in your marriage, put it all on top of the table, not under the table. Iron it out; work it out." (No divorce unless physical abuse threatens one's health or life.)
4. Bishop A. Dewey William, my pastor, during my teen years, said: "As a child of GOD, you are to represent Him every day and in every way. You heed His teachings rather than what everybody else is saying, doing, wearing or going. Remember, you are a child of GOD!"
5. Seth Ballard, Jr., my oldest brother advised me once when I was angry, very angry with Momma or Dad. He said: "Jannie, ("Kisser"), don't let Momma and Dad make you so angry that you do or say something disrespectful that you will regret for the rest of your life. Take a deep breath. Wait it out."
6. Daisy Ballard Cobbins, a younger sister said: "If your problem can be solved with a dollar (money), it's not too serious."
7. Elder Lem Johnson: My God-sent husband has supported my vision for over 25 years. He sacrificed personal Pastor's Anniversary funds to pay the start-up fees for Caring n'

Sharing School and has worked beside me and before me as, husband, advisor and School Board Chairman.

8. School: "Do all you can as if your success depends all on you! And, trust God as if it all depends on Him."
9. Dr. Laurence C. Jones, President of Piney Woods School said: "Work as if everything depends on you, and Pray as if everything depends on God."
10. Mamie Ballard Crockett, my youngest sister said: "If you cannot answer a request with a *yes* or *no*, say, "Let me think about that and get back with you later." Avoid sharing all your explanations and excuses at that time."
11. Mrs. Alicia Jefferson said: "As a leader, there will be times you must make hard calls; make some tough decisions. It comes with the territory."
12. Mrs. Bessie Rozelle, my aunt said: "Jannie, don't spend all your money at any *sale,* no matter how great. There will always be other sales." ---

Children Can Learn to Live and Stay Out of Trouble

Regardless of all the bad reports about youngsters, I know that they don't have to be bad. They do what they have learned to do or what they believe to be okay to do.

Today, youngsters aren't so inclined to close their mouths, listen and learn from their elders. Why? They feel no need or purpose to listen. They have no fear of any consequences of pain. So, they push to the limit, until the talking time is up.

If we are to get control again, if the children are to learn how to live, stay out of trouble and be winners, we'll have to detoxify their minds of meaningless messages, violent entertainment and daily exposure to sexual immorality. Then prayerfully, we have to start the process of re-programming their minds with life rules and guidelines for living with self and others.

Children need help that works. We can do it.

The Caring n' Sharing School in Madison,
MS where we focus on the truth. #1
(11-3-08)

———————◆◆◆———————

"Bits of Wisdom" from Our Classroom

1. The rules of life remain the same.
2. Life has no meaning without its specifics.
3. Self-discipline is the best discipline; self-help is the best help in the long Run.

© Caring n' Sharing, '13-'14

Fools' Hill

Have you heard the statement that children will go up "fools' hill"? I think to myself, is that the only hill of choice or not?

If there is a fools' hill, there has to be another hill that's not fools' hill.

My point is? Let's not assume that our children will go up fools' hill just because others have or because we also went. Behavior is personal; it does not have to be a duplicate. If we expect children to go up fools' hill, they will be inclined to believe us and might feel obliged to fulfill our expectations.

When we look back over our lives, we might have chosen to go up fools' hill but that was our personal experience. That does not have to be the blueprints for our children or for any child to follow.

So, when we teach children let's remember to teach them in the way they should go rather than in the foolish way we might have gone. Okay?

--- Caring n' Sharing School, Madison, #3

Let your head rule your emotions; not your emotions rule your head. ---Lucile Ballard

(Mother of Jannie Johnson)

Our Bodies Are to Be Temples of God

God said that our bodies are to be temples. We live in them and He desires to live in them, too. Therefore, our temples are to be kept pure/clean. He said that He will NOT dwell/live in unclean temples.

If we believe what God said, and what He said matters to us, then we will hear and heed His words. If He said that He will NOT dwell/live in unclean temples, that means if we want to please Him, we have to live up to His standard of morality.

We might choose to make exceptions. We might choose to be more compassionate and understanding in these modern times. But God has said that He changes NOT. Whatever He said long, long ago is still true today for Him and His children.

If we are believers, we want our behavior to reflect what God has said. We will choose to live up to His standard. We will refrain from sexual sins, drunkenness, lying, cheating, stealing and anything that is contrary to what He has said and what He has commanded.

Pleasing Him is our priority!

-- Caring n' Sharing School, Madison, #4

"Bits of Wisdom" From Our Class

STAND TALL and ERECT as a person of integrity: STRONG, HONEST, TRUE and God-fearing. Purpose in your heart that you will NOT bend, bow, buckle, stoop or yield but STAND!
You are FREE ... yes, free indeed!

Being a teenager is a challenge. It was a challenge for me, too, back in that day. It was a bitter, sweet time in my life. I enjoyed the newness of life, all the firsts of this and that. Temptations were great and tempting back then, too.

Looking back, I think what made my experience seem easier, than now, was that I knew what to do and what to say. I had been taught the reasons for my dos and don'ts, all my growing up years. Reasons, reasons were a part of my constitution.

So, for me, it mattered not how good a boy looked or how much I felt I loved him, I knew I was not married. Therefore, certain behavior didn't belong in my life, if I wanted to be considered a good girl, a Christian girl. That was important to me!

So, I was not opened for debate, discussion or opinions, I knew what was proper, decent and moral. My choice was and is today, to heed and obey God's word.

God helped me and kept me. He is still in the helping and keeping business for all who believe.

Cn'S School, Madison, MS #5

Kenya came to Cn'S when she was fifth grade.
Kenya Johnson is now a 2020 College Graduate who still volunteers and visits the school to encourage other boys and girls.

Your Source Will Be with You

Everybody needs to have a source for definitions, reasons, and understanding about what is right for his or her behavior as to what, when, how and with whom.

Some of us might go to relatives, friends, or our pastors. Some of us choose to go to God as our Source and final authority. If we go to people, regardless of their positions, we need to realize that people change their minds, shift their beliefs and viewpoint.

Therefore, I recommend a sure Source, a dependable Source, one that shall never change or die, that source is God. He promised that He will never leave nor forsake us. That's the kind of assurance and dependability we need in times like these.

–Caring n' Sharing School, Madison, #6

"Bit of Wisdom" from Our Classroom

Fit your life to the truth, rather than fit the truth to your life.

One of our recent governors supported abstinence. I appreciate that; I am glad he believes that youngsters can abstain. I do, too. Why not?

But, if we are going to push this, we adults have to get ourselves together as to what we want youngsters to see, hear, believe and heed. Sharing a good idea or expressing our desire for them might not be convincing enough. They have to have personal reasons beyond our talk and hoping.

Along with good information, youngsters need personal reasons for resisting the temptations of being sexually active. If we, their teachers, first, can see them as temples, unique, original, one-of-a-kind, we can better help them to see themselves as special, unique, one of a kind. Because, they are, they should NOT lower that standard to please somebody's desire or submit to their own fleshly desires.

However, if we talk favorably for both abstaining and not abstaining, youngsters will most likely choose the one with less discipline and/or the choice of their friends. The choice of *abstinence* has to be the one of honor and the other choice is one of dishonor. If the distinction is not made clear, youngsters will be confused. Let's remember that the matter of sex is a moral issue, too. God is the Source, the Reference Point for determining what is moral and immoral. He said that sex outside of marriage is sin. (I Corinthians 6:13-20) He calls it fornication. He has not changed or altered His moral standard.

Caring n' Sharing School, Madison, MS #7

Warning Signs Should be Heeded

You have a body of your own, a life of your own and a mind of your own. You can make some decisions for YOURSELF. Remember, do right because it is right to do right. That's good sense. –Jannie Johnson

Sometime ago, I went to Canton for jury duty. I drove at about forty-five for twenty uninterrupted minutes on Hwy 55. On the way, I noticed a trailer house being pulled by a tractor. On the front of the trailer was a big sign, "Oversized load." Flickering yellow lights and little red flags were on the corners of the trailer house. Closely behind was a small pickup truck with lights and flags, too.

I said to myself, those lights, flags, big sign are for our safety. Somebody saw the need and cared enough to do what was needed for highway safety.We need moral courage to tell young folks what's needed for safety on the highway of life.

Radio Spot, #8
Caring n' Sharing School

↗ One Way ↗

Life is a one-time, one-way experience. We never become experts at life because our lives keep moving on and on with time.

If sound principles are learned and practiced, consistently, they will put us in good standing for living.

How does one know the principles of life? They are generally rulings that are true for all mankind, regardless of race, creed, color, time or location.

To live or not to live by principles is a choice. Nevertheless, those choices are very important. They will determine much of the quality to be experienced in life.

My father once said, "By the time one learns how to live, it's time to die." There's a lot of truth in his statement. Therefore, early on we need to learn the basic principles of life. We have to allow ourselves to learn from others who have lived, learned and succeeded in life.

We do not have to learn everything first hand. We can allow ourselves to learn from others. Some say that experience is the best teacher. I have since learned that depends on: What's the experience or lesson? Who's the learner and, who's example is demonstrated in the lesson to be learned?

The answers to those questions will determine whether an experience is a good teacher and whether that lesson was a good lesson to be learned or not.

Think about that. Okay?

Cn'S of Madison, MS, #10

Expensive to Communicate

As we shift from a common source in America, it is getting harder and harder to communicate. It is getting expensive just to do what we used to do for free or at a minimum cost. Today, what we think we have fixed or settled have a way of popping up again, later, in a lawsuit.

We can say one thing and mean another; we have become careless in our words and what our words imply.

We forget the promises we made. We are preoccupied with other interests at the time we make them. We change our minds about vows and feel no need to keep them anymore. We say we are tired.

This happens in many marriages. Promises are made at the altar before many witnesses, gifts are received and honeymoon is yet to be paid. Before the wedding presents are opened and put away, the bride and groom are forgetting and breaking their vows and promises.

I've heard some say, "I don't love him/her any more. I didn't marry for this! I ask, what happened to that part of the marriage vows that said 'for better or worse'?

God said let your *yea* be *yea* and your *nay* be *nay*. Remember?

Caring n' Sharing School of Madison, #11

The Creation: What Do You Believe?

Every once in a while, I hear the old question about which comes first, the chicken or the egg?

Well ... I answer that question with a question. **Do you believe in the creation or what?**

If you believe in the creation, then the answer is the chicken came first. During those 6 days of creation, God said let there be and that's good. Did He ever say let there be eggs?

We discuss back and forth the creation and evolution. I finally found a way to put that debate to rest in me.

I was not here for the creation. I was not here for the big bang, the beginning of the evolution theory. Were you?

Since we were not here, we have no living witnesses, either. Therefore, it's our choice to believe or not to believe the creation story in the Bible or the evolution theory of some scientists.

With or without evidence or proof, to believe or not to believe is still a matter of choice. I choose to believe the creation story of the Bible.

Caring n' Sharing School
Madison, MS #12

About God

As we Americans drift away from God, who has been our Source of common definitions, shared understandings and general expectations, what and who will be The Almighty, All-knowing and Everywhere Source?

How will we determine what is right or wrong? What is good or evil? What is fair or just? In disputes, when we have done all we know to do, who can we trust to settle the matter sooner or later. Who can make us feel no need to get revenge or get even, period!

Our push for separation, as if there is no common ground to be found, and our individualistic attitudes have created new, and unfamiliar circumstances for us in our desire and effort to have a civil society. We cannot expect a civil society if the citizens have no reasons within to be civil. Our laws are limited in their power. Though they are intended for the good of the people, they are losing power everyday as we, the citizens lose respect for the Giver of power, God.

Caring n' Sharing School, Madison, MS #13

"Bits of Wisdom" from Our Class

If you praise, start with others. If you criticize, start with yourself.
If you have problems to solve, do your best then trust God for the rest.

The Bird in Hand

Have you heard the old saying, "One bird in hand is better than 2 in the bush?"

That statement can mean different things to different folks. But, to me a simple meaning would be, don't let go of what you have in hopes of what you might get.

In other words, go slow before you let go. Count up the cost; consider the circumstance now and possibly later. Ask yourself some "what if" questions. If things go as you desire and what if things do not go as you anticipate.

Let's remember that failure is just as real as success. It's a fact, failure is next door to success. Even though we are positive people and feel very hopeful, sometimes things just have a way of going the other way. Therefore, let's make haste slowly and prayerfully.

Caring n' Sharing School, Radio spot, #14

———◆◆◆———

People want to change your mind about the
truth so they can change you.
-- Jannie Johnson

Praise Should Be Earned

The worth of life is not in years alone, but in deeds done while living. –Jannie Johnson

If praise is given regardless of shoddy work, tardiness, abuse of work time and company supplies, THEN that praise is without substance, with little or no value.

Praise is like pay, like money, reward for a job well done. Praise is to be earned.

A job well done, it's superior. This is not well done only in the eyes and judgment of the one to be praised. But, rather it's the decision of the one who gives the praise.

The work efforts have to be praise worthy, beyond the call of duty, more than what is expected or required in the job description. Praise is not to be asked for or demanded.

So, those of us who are working should do praise worthy work. Those of us who observe or are aware of excellent work should show appreciation with praise, bonuses, etc.

To praise or not to praise, starts with the worker, the doer, the student rather than with the boss, teacher or person to give the praise.

Again, praiseworthiness comes before the reward of praise. But there is an art to giving praise. I don't claim to have mastered it. But I do know about its diminishing returns.

Charles Kendall Adams said that "No one ever attains very eminent success by simply doing what is required of him; it is the **amount and the excellence of what is over and beyond the required that determines the greatness of distinction.** So, it's the *over and beyond* that is to get the praise. Again, praise is to come with and for the extra that's done.

---- Caring n' Sharing School, Madison, MS #15

World Government or Global Government?

A few weeks ago, I was on a radio Talk Show. The host asked me to give my thoughts on a quote written by Brock Adams, director of UN Health Organization. This is the quote:

"To achieve world government, it is necessary to remove from the minds of men their individualism, loyalty to family traditions, national patriotism, and religious dogmas."

I responded with questions. I asked, if we subtract individualism, loyalty to family traditions, national patriotism and religious dogmas, what will be left? What will hold people together as individuals, as a family, and as a nation? Why will or why would anybody care about himself, his family, the nation or anything?

How can we motivate or inspire each other to get up and do right? We know what has worked in the past. We know where we came from and have come through.

Do we want to cut out all that which distinguishes us as individuals and as a nation, to achieve what? Global government, what's that; what does that look like? Now is the time to think about the direction we are drifting/going. Okay?

---Caring n' Sharing School, Madison, MS #16

- 15 -

Letters with Lessons

Diverse skin color is like using the whole box of permanent markers.
---Mamie Crockett

The youngest at Cn'S

Dear Granddaughters,

I commend you for finding reasons, year after year, to stay in school and graduate with a high school diploma. Now my question is are you ready for the classroom in the bigger world?

This fall, on your college campus, you'll meet professors and students of different races, religions, lifestyles, attitudes and backgrounds. That's a different world than your home training and home schooling.

I think you'll do all right in college if you stay focused on who you are and *why* you are there.

Well ... you know how I value education, particularly teaching. But, I'm not blind to what I see neither deaf to the things I hear. I've been teaching and learning a long time. I **know** what works best in life for the long run.

You will be learning from your professors and schoolmates but your purpose for college is to continue your education NOT to find yourself. You "found" yourself at home along with your name, your race, sex, birthday, parents and place of birth. That information is also on your birth certificate. Check it out.

You're single, so behave as if you are. A boyfriend is just that a **boyfriend** not a **husband**. You might meet some professors and students who **don't know** the difference **or** don't respect that difference. That's ... on ... them. Don't you play dumb; you know better; you know the difference.

Back in the day, I lived on a campus. So, I have some experience. I know dorm mates can be informative and very persuasive. Upper classmen can seem so smart and cool. Don't get fooled by them; stay focused on your life for the now AND the later.

Your formal education is **NOT to replace** your common sense. So, keep your head. Before you started school, you learned to take a bath, put on clean clothes, tuck in your blouse, comb your hair, tie-up your shoes, snap your snaps, button your buttons, zip your zippers, eat your food and brush your teeth before going out in public. Remember?

In preschool, you learned to mark and write on paper and chalk boards NOT on your body. You were taught to cherish your body as precious, special, and valuable. It's your temple where you live and where God wants to live, too. So, don't poke holes in it or its parts. If you must poke holes, poke them in the flower beds in my backyard.

Loosely cover your nakedness. What's moral or ethical in revealing your *everything*: your skinniness, fatness, curves, cracks, or other seductive areas? Why flaunt your **beauty** before some lustful minds and eyes that dwell on the possibility of disrobing you? Don't entice behavior that is not good for you. Be a LADY of integrity with dignity! Respect yourself and demand that others do the same.

Granddaughter, stay focused on your purpose at college. Enjoy, yes; have fun, **if** you can but **NOT** in exchange for your common sense and decency. You might be tempted to compromise but don't you bend, bow, buckle, stoop or yield. STAND!! You can, yes you can!

We your family, relatives and friends trust you to do right and go straight. We expect you to be trustworthy. Okay?

Start now to pray for yourself, your professors, and school mates. Plan to study much, do your schoolwork, be on time for class and mind your own business. If at any time you sense doubting in your faith or begin questioning the reality in principle living, call me. I'll be somewhere listening and praying for you.

Love you,
Your Big Momma
Jannie B. Johnson
Call me; I'll answer.

Dear Grandson,

You might not want to read this letter, but go ahead and read it anyhow. It's not a bad letter. It's a letter about a few things that I think can help you OR can hinder you in life.

If you ask me what I think will be your greatest temptation, I would say **ly**-ing, not being truthful. Lying can be done in words, deeds and motives. Lies can be labeled as *white* lies, big and little or bold-faced lies. But, lies are lies by any name or color. So, from the start, don't deal in lies nor give way to foolishness. Be truthful even though at times it might NOT seem possible or appreciated, be truthful, anyhow.

Let me tell you why I like the truth. I like it because it does not change for race, creed, location or the times. Truth is what it **is** with or without approval. It is what it **was** and it is what it's **going** to be. Think about that ...

Truth is important, a necessity for life and living. There's NO justice without truth. Courts cannot function without truth, so help us God. Victims cry for it and the Lord demands it.

Lies kill relationships; make solutions impossible, defeat justice, make contracts, wills and documents worthless and business deals invalid.

Don't be a hypocrite, living a lie. That's so low class and disrespectful. Choose to be truthful to yourself and to others in all your dealings. Choose to be an honest man, a gen-tle-man of honor with respect and integrity!

Are you following me?

I speak NOT as an expert but as your Big Momma. I love you and want you to do right and go straight. I want you to live your life according to the principles of life and connect to others who are of the same mind and embrace the truth, too.

Grandson, resist the temptation to compromise to that level of what's acceptable, expedient or everybody else is doing it. Foolishness can seem like fun in the NOW when there are no apparent consequences but it can be **embarrassing** in the later. The only kept-secrets are the ones NOT made.

Believe me when I say a little bit can hurt. You can get addicted. Somebody can find out and tell on you, too. You can end up in a bad place or killed. Yes, my dear, that little cute girlfriend will get pregnant, sooner or later, *if you two choose to do that which makes babies.*

*You **cannot** undo an experience, good or bad.*

Some ten plus years ago, grandson, you were born to your parents. Your coming-out experience was witnessed and documented. Your parents received a copy of it in the form of a birth certificate. It has your name, your birthday, **your sex**, your parents' name, your birth place and your time of birth. You might want to change a thing or two on your birth certificate. But the truth is **what it is** with or without your liking or approval. The truth can stand without defense.

Truth is like that!

If you choose to re-define truth according to your feelings and opinions, you'll be tempted to do it again and again. To have stability in your life, you need to keep your faith in God who changes NOT. He is the Source of the truth. You'll learn on your life's journey that you need God, the Source of truth to give you purpose and meaning for life and to create in you a feeling of self-worth and self-esteem. You'll need strength to live by convictions and courage to tell the truth.

In a few more years, you'll **be legal**. That means you will be free to make some choices without parental consent. Don't be fooled by the label "legal." Legal can be good/bad, fair/unfair, moral or immoral. If you want to check out your legal rights, go ahead. But, before **you do** something illegal, unnatural or immoral, ask yourself is this the behavior of a young Christian man. You know the difference and there should be distinctions. Tell the **truth,** son.

You'll meet some adults, teachers and peers who have

different views about what's right and wrong and what's normal and abnormal. They might even have different attitudes toward certain habits, lifestyles and living arrangements. Dare to **think for yourself!** Don't be afraid to think NO matter how sensitive the subject.

I might have told you this before but allow me to repeat myself. Okay? There are three sets of laws: man's, nature's and God's. Man's laws determine what is legal and illegal. Nature's laws determine what is normal and abnormal. God's laws determine what is right and wrong, moral and immoral.

From time to time, some folks might claim to have discovered **something new** or have found **another way** to think, believe and behave. Well ... remember the truth is what it is. It has no respect of persons neither regards for anybody's feelings or opinions.

So, don't allow yourself to be hoodwinked and bamboozled by the fluff and stuff of today. Stick with the truth, God's truth. It has weathered the storms of life and stood the test of time. Don't ... fight it, just respect it and be happy. Okay?

Love you,
Big Momma, Jannie B. Johnson

———◆———

No one ever experiences lack as a result
of sharing. —Mamie Crockett

Precious Ones,

Come now, let's think it through and talk it out. It's time …

If you have a family with married parents who are honest, hardworking and caring, you are blessed, indeed blessed. This should be a good time in your life. You are young, full of life and ideas. Nothing is hurting you and everything is working. WOW! This has to be g-o-o-d!

Do you feel invincible? My mother would say, "Don't let feelings fool you. Life has its common denominator. It has a way of keeping you mindful that from the dust you came and to the dust you shall return."

Think about this, you have one body, just one. It has to last you a lifetime. If it gets sick, you are sick. If you use drugs or do something outrageous that will hurt your body or cause it to die, you will hurt or die, too.

Why, because you live in your body. You cannot live without it and it cannot live without you. Therefore, you must keep your body healthy and safe if you want to live a long time.

Be particular about your body as to what you allow your ears to hear, your eyes to see, what enters your mouth/body and with whom you associate.

It matters yes, it matters! Be jealous about who you are and whose you are. I am. I'm jealous for you because I know how valuable you are for now and later. I hurt when I see how you markup your body with tattoos as if you are a chalkboard, canvas, or some disposable material.

What notion gave you the idea that it's a sign of intelligence to poke holes in your body: nose, lip, tongue, belly button, etc.? Who are you allowing to influence your thinking and to shape your beliefs? What are your opinions about what it means for you to be your best, do your best and to look your best?

Precious ones, life has rules and standards. Life has not changed; the rules/standards are the same. Life makes no allowances for your, "I think, I feel, everybody else is …" rationales. If you choose to break the rules, you suffer the sin, shame, and disgrace of it. If you dare to ignore life's principles, your family and those who love you will hurt and suffer with you.

Remember also, drugs are not afraid of you;
so, you have to be afraid of them. –JJ

Yes, you are a promise, a possibility and a life of potentiality. Living a principle-centered life should not be boring for you. It's the way of life for the noble and free. That's you!

Keep Dreaming, Keep Thinking … I'm Jannie Johnson

———————◆◆◆———————

Learn to be satisfied with the truth as the final authority.

From "Bits of Wisdom," Caring n' Sharing

Dear Students,

At your age, you might feel no need to read what I am writing. But at my age, I feel a need to write something, (while the blood still runs warm in my veins).

I know you have a lot of voices calling for your mind and attention. You have that awesome responsibility to hear and heed the right calling. The choice you make can be life changing and future altering for you.

I feel for you and I feel with you, too. You are young with limited knowledge and limited experience. So, you have to trust somebody to help steer you in your choice of actions. Your choosing the right somebody could be like gambling, playing a game of chance not with money but your life and your future.

Listen, precious ones, the journey of life is too long for shallow thinking. Take time and make your moves slowly and prayerfully.

I am going to say something about folks that you might not have thought about before. Folks can be good and bad, dumb and smart, honest and dishonest. Sometimes it's all mixed up and lopsided, too. Some folks have purpose and direction for their lives and others just DON'T have a clue. They live by trial and error not by principles.

Folks for the most part, look normal, talk and act very much alike. But you have to listen to determine whether they respect their own words or not. Listen for their meaning and their point of reference: God, a sense of what's right, fair and just. If folks don't have respect for the truth, they can't communicate clearly and honestly on any particular subject.

There are distinctions between legal and illegal, normal and abnormal, right and wrong. You'll learn soon if not already, that we adults can do and say some non-sen-si-cal things. For example, we'll claim to be for what's legally right and morally sound until we experience personal conflict. Then, we will make new policies and rewrite old laws to accommodate our bad habits and immoral lifestyles.

Students, our thinking might be politically correct and our

behavior understandable but know this, everything that is legal is NOT right and everything that is right is not legal.

Don't be afraid to think for yourself no matter how sensitive the subject. Sexuality is a very sensitive topic and emotions can kidnap common sense in an instant. Sex is serious, serious business. It's the ONLY human behavior that can limit your freedom, alter your future, take your health, take your life or make new life.

You might not want to admit it but an unwed teen pregnancy can bring guilt, shame, disgrace, regrets, tears and much sorrow to a family, to the young mother and father as well as to the innocent child.

Sex is NOT necessary to sustain human life but sex is necessary to maintain the human race. Wait until you are married to help maintain the human race. It's worth the wait when you can properly care for a new life.

Think about that!

Be **selective** in the activities you allow yourself to enjoy. Be **particular** about the folks you date and the folks with whom you choose to associate. Be **protective** of your mind and your physical body. You cannot undo an experience be it good or bad. Again, be protective, selective and particular about your mind and your body.

Self-discipline is the best discipline in the long run. So, be a personal friend to yourself and your family. That's good business. It's the cool thing to do in these social-media times of **personal choice**, *no sin, no shame and no disgrace.*

Love you for now and forever, precious ones. I'm counting on you to do right and go straight, re-e-e-gardless!!!

Caring n' Sharing, Aug, 21, 2014

Precious Ones:

Come now, precious ones, let's think it through and talk it out. It's time … This is my fifth keepsake letter in my series to you. I want to talk to you about life in general and life in particular.

I define life as the most dangerous game you will have to play. I say game because life has rules/regulations you must follow to be a winner. It is dangerous in that if you choose NOT to learn or follow the rules and regulations, you will suffer and those who love you will suffer, too.

Life is a have-to-game because you didn't ask to be born, nobody did. Nevertheless, you are here and now you are expected to be civil, responsible and productive, too.

To ensure your success, we the taxpayers have put some institutions and services in place to prepare you for life's challenges. Don't take them for granted; they are for you.

My third definition of life is that it is the space of time between birth and death. How long is a life? We do not know. But we do know how many hours in a day and how many months in a year. This is true for the rich, the famous, the poor and the unknown, alike. Life is one way, no U turns, backing up, trading or swapping it out. It's your personal onward, forward journey for better or for worse.

What's my point? Thanks for thinking! It's time for you to give up the attitude of blame, stop the fussing and the fighting with yourselves. It is time to think matters through and talk them out, instead. It's time to think about what is good for you AND others, in the *now* and in the *later.*

We adults who are providing your shelter, food and clothing are not perfect, as you already know, but neither are you. This too, we already know.

We love you; well … we think we do. We hope you love us back or at least respect us for our efforts. Think … we have just one life to live. Why should we make it hard on each other? We need one another, believe me. Life has a way of making us to know, every now and then, that we need folks and we certainly need FAMILY.

You are in the driver's seat of your life; you determine your daily and final destination.

--Jannie Johnson

Dear Precious Ones,

Remember that these letters are for you, for your consideration, and your safekeeping.

I can imagine that you can remember a statement or some statements your mother, father or grandparents have said over and over. You wonder why they feel a need to repeat themselves word for word. However, now you have come to expect to hear those same words whenever you are in their presence. In the words of my mom, "Live on. You'll see."

All my life, for as long as I can remember, my father would say, after one of his *do-right-go-straight* sessions. "You'd better listen to me 'cause I'm goin' to leave here!"

"Where are you going, Dad?" I asked. He answered, "To the grave, and then my talking days will be over." My response was, " ah-ah-h Dad," you say that all the time. "Live on, you'll see," he would say as he was moving about his chores.

Well, I lived on and about thirty years later, I saw Dad on his sick bed. I then remembered what he had said about leaving here. I said, "Dad, tell me about life. What works and what does not work?"

With his eyes closed, his upper lip tucked in and with an unhurried voice he said, "Life is like a circle that goes round and round, one generation after another. The secret to life, the secret to success in life is determined by how well you know the truth, how much you allow truth, absolute truth to shape and guide your attitude and your behavior in the Circle of Life."

Now another thirty years later, I have nothing new to add. It is true, sooner or later you, young ones, will be filling our spaces in the Circle of Life. Truth is the best constant to transcend the generations. Live on, you will see. Young folks need faith, love, honesty, loyalty, integrity and lifestyles that reflect a code of ethics above and beyond popular opinion.

Caring n' Sharing (January 2009)

-16-

Epilogue: Playing It Forward

Silence is not always golden; it can be hurtful if wrongs are unheeded.
—Mamie Crockett

My thinking mind does not allow me to sit and do nothing. For almost twenty years prior to opening Caring n' Sharing school in 1996 at the current location, I was writing mini-lessons for radio and television. I was speaking to thousands of students in several school districts, one of which was an urban school district of more than 30,000 students. Then, I was invited to write as a newspaper columnist for the Clarion-Ledger with a major southern distribution base. It became obvious that participating in different community services, I needed a larger location beyond the current space at home.

Therefore, my husband and I consulted with my mother Lucile who remarried after being widowed for about ten years. The family's old home place-- encompassing the original one-room school, was now vacant. Momma was pleased to have it used for a worthy cause. Following the zoning guidelines for Madison, the school was approved with limited services for this location.

Thus, the Johnson Ministries was established embracing a component called Caring n' Sharing School of Preventive Counseling. This was our expanded response to the needs of children and families throughout several states. We noticed changes in the attitude of students toward *doing right and going straight.*

To date, after twenty-five years of service at this location, parents and grandparents from neighboring communities in Mississippi have brought children to the Cn'S school to hear the unrefined frankness about life and living in the *back then*, the *now* and *the later*.

I firmly believe that NO child has to be bad OR wants to be bad. I really believe that children can learn to live principle-centered lives and be happy, too. To ensure that some enrolled students stay on the right track, I have become the "alarm clock" too by calling them early so they won't be late getting to school or missing the bus. This monitoring is done even though Cn'S is a week-end school held only on Thursdays for two one-hour sessions, 5 to 7 PM and on first and third Saturdays for three one-hour sessions, 9 AM to 12 Noon. Courtesy calls are made two nights before meeting dates to encourage attendance.

Spreading the Word
(1984)

After becoming a columnist for the Clarion-Ledger, I had a larger platform from which to address issues that youth and families face. I wrote an article that appeared in the Clarion-Ledger during that season. The behavior was problematic, but the solution—though not simple—was doable. The message is about the same today. I wish to share an excerpt because it describes the past, present and possible future goals of the Caring n' Sharing School.

Like Aesop, a clever Greek slave, wanted to point out immorality in his day, I want to point out the same in my day. However, both of us wanted to avoid hurting the feelings of the proud and great. In Aesop's day, that would have meant cruel punishment for him. I, too, want to teach moral principles in my lessons without making folks mad at me. Therefore, I use my hand puppet.

Whereas Aesop's fables used talking-animals as characters in his stories to make a point, I use "T. C." (Tough Cooky), a hand puppet, to explain the seriousness of life with its joys and sorrows. My objective is to cause students to think about their behavior and the positive or negative consequences for their choices.

My childhood dream was to be a scholar, an intellectual. I always admired folks who were knowledgeable, had strong minds and clear vision, clear hearts, good health, unyielding love and peace. They were about something worthy of emulation! They had learned the art of living.

I went to school every day, listened to my teachers and did my schoolwork. I kept my hands and feet to myself. I was a good student but not a scholar. My childhood environment was restricted, resources limited and opportunities few. My diversity was a hindrance.

Within my child's mind, I tried to figure out why Americans would plot and plan laws as ways to hinder fellow Americans from their inalienable rights to life, liberty and the pursuit of happiness. The adults in my community did not have the answers. They, too, were asking why.

My dad answered it in this way: "Ignorance is the darkness of the mind. In darkness, man will hurt himself and others. He cannot see." My dad dared to think above and beyond his circumstances. His boldness encouraged me and sacred me too.

In those "why," and "how come" days, I was afraid my dad would get killed or be compelled to leave home, relocate, like his father, Nelson Ballard. I was afraid that our house would be burned or bombed while we were asleep or away. I was afraid that our land would be taken like my great grandfather's 300 acres. I was afraid.

I had no confidence in the laws. Justice that reached our

community was not blind. I was afraid of policemen. I did not know them as persons who were "to serve and protect."

Growing up and being surrounded by scary experiences can put wrinkles in a child's mind, mental dendrites, that ripple on and on. I know; I have memories that are freeze-dried in my mind. They ripple like a pebble thrown in a lake of water; they continue. Those ripples, no doubt, form the motivation for what I do today as a preventive counselor.

I hold the plumb-line so boys and girls can learn how to stay out of trouble and be about something GOOD, unless it's "good trouble" like the late Congressman John Lewis employed.

I have not made the Who's Who List of great people, but I have learned some What's What. Diversity is nothing new. It is as old as "In the beginning." Diversity is not superior to unity. Unity holds relationships, institutions and civilizations together. Political correctness can strip us of our natural identities and make us clones in too many ways.

I am not a scholar but I KNOW that the "playing field" is TOO level when and where the following are acceptable:

- Incorrect English is acceptable everywhere, including schools;
- Profanity is in style;
- Disrespect is comedy;
- Dressing "down" is encouraged [everywhere];
- Sex is considered a matter of orientation, personal choice or lifestyle and
- Truth is relative.

In this *now-now* time, let us Americans not stand by *speechlessly*, afraid of our thoughts about those who use the Constitution as a cloak for their selfishness, greed and immorality. Tolerance does not mean "do nothing" about behavior that destroys and hinders freedom.

Now, I will ask the same question Langston Hughes asked: "What happens to a dream unfulfilled: Does it wither like a raisin, fester like a sore or becomes a heavy bothersome load?" I sensed the answer to this question during the February 2020 Founder's Day Program in which the parents urged attendees to ensure that my dream for Caring n' Sharing School does not become a heavy bothersome load. Therefore, they encouraged each other to support the school financially.

That day, the packed 104-year-old all-purpose classroom was showing signs of inadequacy as the satisfied clientele moved around or turned sideways so that students could weave by to make speeches or parents to make encouraging remarks and give testimonies. The consensus was that ten more years of the "Do right, go straight" teachings could help another generation of very capable, promising youth.

Therefore, it is the vision of the staff, parents, partners and Board of the Caring n' Sharing School of Preventive Counseling that the philosophy of doing right, and doing what it takes (including making personal sacrifices) the school will continue for generations to come.

Boys and girls of Caring n' Sharing School
with Jannie Johnson (2012)

Where there is no vision, the people perish. Proverbs 29:18

Christ Missionary and Industrial College (founded initially in 1897 and charted in 1907) is an example of a dream drying up like a raisin. I worked at my church-sponsored school teaching the *Do Right, Go Straight principles*. I did not attend CM&I, but my father did. Also, our son, Lemzel, attended and my husband taught there for two years.

Even though I am not an alumnus, I caught the CM&I passion. With or without pay, but with gusto, I taught at CM&I part-time for over thirty years. Why? Because I wanted to be fair with my fellow sisters and brothers who were trying to carry the whole load. I realized that it's my responsibility to represent myself as a Christian in action. It is my responsibility to make sure that the work I do *speaks well for me. Now is our time, our only time.*

The sad part about the story of CM&I is that it was closed in 2017 due to inadequate funds and "relevance" in the community. In 1897, Mrs. Alice Brown saw the need for an institution to educate the head, heart and hands of boys and girls. Her vision was realized and continued for over 100 consecutive years. The church leaders, at that time, embraced her vision and bought 244 acres of land in 1906 at market value. They built the school building on it, at market cost, without financial aid from the city, state or whatever. (However, there were no financial support systems for African Americans other than their personal resources.)

As a National Missionary of the Church of Christ Holiness (USA), I am ashamed to think that, today, we have more opportunities, more resources and more know-how than our fore parents but yet we do less to keep afloat a school like Christ Missionary and Industrial College. Some caring people appear to have less to give, less time and little mind to care.

This is why my husband and I feel compelled to care at the Caring n' Sharing School (a.k.a. Johnson Ministries) and thank God that we still have community support to keep the school going for this and the next generation.

Jannie Johnson and Elder Lem Johnson of Caring n' Sharing School

At the Caring n' Sharing School, the helm is a directional symbol. It's a reminder that God wants to hold the helm of our lives. If God is the Captain, we can trust Him to steer us through troubled waters.

APPENDICES

∞Celebrating 25 Years
(1994-2019)
∞Bits of Wisdom

Attendees Celebrating Founder's Day
Left to Right: Ethel Brashears, Raquel
Marion-Milton, Jannie Johnson,
Jo Ann Johnson, Mamie B. Crockett, and Lemzel Johnson

Celebrating 25 Years of Service
Children are our Mission.
Education is our business.
Teaching is our specialty.
Prevention is our priority.
Truth is our focus.
Conversation is our method.
Honesty is our policy.
The Golden Rule is our *Rule*.
Family is our style.
Love is our emotion.
Faithfulness is our call.
"Yes," is our answer.
God is our Source, and now is our Time

1. Man's mind is too small to disagree with God who knows it all.
2. Your conscience is not the final authority for ethical conduct/behavior.
3. Beliefs and behavior are conjoined.
4. Keeping up in life is not for the slothful, lazy or unconcerned.
5. History cannot be unlived but it can be relived.
6. Truth can take the scary out of life.
7. Truth goes where it is invited; stays where it is respected; blesses and multiplies where it is remembered and practiced.
8. To change from good to evil is not noble. To change from evil to good is noble.
9. Bad things can happen if there is not any opposition.
10. You are not programmed by nature to think automatically.
11. Teaching can be abstract and far removed from where you live your daily life that you cannot relate.
12. Regardless of the who, what, when or where you are, behave yourself in such a manner that will not cause you to be a victim in the *now* or ashamed in the *later*.
13. Talk to yourself in unspoken words in declarative, imperative, interrogative and exclamatory statements.
14. You can like people and like having them around but do not allow them to be the determining factors as to what is right and wrong for your life.
15. Your behavior is YOUR responsibility: it's your choosing, your doing, your fault; you permitted it. Therefore, the consequences are yours, too!
16. Be your friend in your thinking, your choosing, your decisions and responsibilities.

© Caring 'N Sharing, '13- '14

If you have problems to solve, do your best then trust God for the rest.

A *Bit of Wisdom* from Our Class

I Repeat here what I believe:

*I, Jannie Ballard Johnson, believe that NO child has to be bad. I believe that youngsters can learn from their mistakes BEFORE they make them. They can learn how to live principle-centered lives and be happy, too. Why not? Knowing **how-to live** is just as important as knowing **how-to make** a living. I know now that experience is NOT always the best teacher and bought sense is NOT always affordable.*

A MORAL DROUGHT PRODUCES STUNTED LIVES.
–JANNIE B. JOHNSON

REFERENCES

Bosch, C. W. 1988. *Bully on the Bus*. (Parenting Press, Inc., Seattle, Washington)

Caring n' Sharing School of Preventive Counseling. 2013—2019. "Bits of Wisdom." (Unpublished Compilation of Proverbs from Students of Jannie Johnson. Used with Permission) Madison, MS

Church, F. P. (1897). "Yes, Virginia, there is a Santa Claus." An editorial, *Sun Newspaper of New York*. *(September 21, 1897)*.

Hill, Sheridan with JoeAnn Ballard. (2014). *Called, How One Couple Served A City*. (Montreat, NC: Real Life Stories)

The Holy Bible 1997. *Authorized King James Version*, (Cornerstone Bible Publishers, Nashville, TN 37234-0164.) Permission requested from Westbow for Hosea 4:6 (paraphrased); Proverbs 22:6 (modified) 1 John 4:4; II Thessalonian 3:10, I Corinthians 6: 9-11, I Corinthians 6:13-29, and I Corinthians 6:18, Proverbs 29:18.)

Jefferson, Anita B. Reunion, *Christ Missionary and Industrial College* (1897-2016). Pp. 28-32; p.68.

146 Johnson, Jannie. "Racial unrest is deeper than ..." *The Clarion-Ledger*, Opinion Section. (July 11, 2015). (Excerpt used with permission).

Johnson, Jannie. (1988). *Preventive Counseling for Practical Living*, Caring n' Sharing with Jannie Johnson. Madison, MS: Johnson Ministries. (Excerpts used with permission).

Johnson, Jannie. (1991). *Caring n' Sharing with Jannie Johnson*. Madison, MS: Johnson Ministries. (Excerpts used with permission).

Kennedy, John F. (1963). (John F. Kennedy Library, TNC:262). Online video documentary.

National Publishing Board. (1977). *His Fullness Songs*. (Church of Christ (Holiness) USA, Jackson, MS 39212, p. 277.

Purcell, L. H. 1956. *Miracle in Mississippi, Laurence C. Jones of Piney Woods. (New York: Carlton Press) pp. 40, 56; 78; 86-87; 209.*

The Old Farmer's Summer Almanac. (2020). Boys Town Publication/ Almanac.com Almanac.com, p. 13.

Thompson, C. D. (1973). *The History of the Mississippi Teachers Association.* (NEA Teachers Rights of Washington, DC. and Mississippi Teachers Association, Jackson, MS) pp.10-22

JANNIE JOHNSON'S BOOKLETS. 8-PIECE SET FOR A DONATION OF $20 OR MORE; 4 PIECE SET FOR A DONATION OF $12, OR $3.00 EACH

Each of Jannie's eight instructional booklets gives a *play-by-play* strategy for the game of life. Mr. Larry Hogue, Supervisor of Educational Services at the Mississippi Power & Light Company evaluates her strategy this way: "I have had the privilege of observing Jannie Johnson in class. She is an effective speaker, able to hold the attention of the elementary students ... Certainly, her message of values is one that needs to be taught today more than ever."

Website: www.caringnsharing.net Call to place orders at Office: 601-856-2611 or 601-856-6755.

Jannie B. Johnson is a newspaper columnist, a teacher, a preventive counselor, a radio and television personality and a certified elementary teacher with cognates in Psychology and Sociology. Over a span of fifty years, she collaborated with five school districts as consultant and motivational speaker. More than 50,000 students have benefited from the principled *Do right, go straight* lifestyle.

Growing up, Mrs. Johnson experienced poverty, harassment and vestiges of racism, but learned to cherish and practice the principle-centered lifestyle and Christian faith that sustained her parents and fore parents. Currently, the same principle-styled teachings have deterred thousands and continue to direct youngsters to "do right and go straight." She believes *no child is born bad or wants to be bad.* Mrs. Johnson is convinced that when society's pathway through life gets cloudy, unfair or crooked, children can and, many times, get lost. Therefore, like the "stern" of a boat, her teachings guide children through the uncharted waters of life. Approximately ninety-five per cent of youngsters (elementary through high school) who attend the Caring n' Sharing School of Preventive Counseling (Madison, MS), for two or more years, change from being probable liabilities to becoming assets in their respective communities. Mrs. Johnson is the wife of Elder Lem Johnson, Jr., mother of one adult son and grandmother of four.

Printed in the United States
by Baker & Taylor Publisher Services